# From Worry to Wonder

## Seeing God's Goodness in Life's Rearview Mirror

Amy Hagerup

My True Stories

# DEDICATION

For my grandchildren:
Tyler, Zachary, Isaac, Elyse, Esther, Judson, Cullen, Seth, Owen, Levi, Gavin, Margee, Ruby, and Archie.

These stories are part of God's legacy for our family. Always remember to love God first and then look for the good that He will accomplish through the trials you encounter. Be sure to share these stories with your children and grandchildren so that God will be glorified for all His wonders in our life. (Psalm 78:4)

I love you,

Nana

# TABLE OF CONTENTS


PREFACE: An Invitation to Change Worry to Wonder ........ 1

SECTION I: GOD'S PROVSION OF EVERY NEED ........ 5

1. Assignment: Loneliness ........ 6

2. Down to My Last Two Dollars ........ 14

3. A Needed Item I Forgot to Bring ........ 18

4. A Powerful Lesson from God's Provision ........ 23

5. No One Can Outgive God! ........ 28

6. Too Exhausted to Serve a Visitor ........ 34

SECTION II: GOD'S PROTECTION IN TRAVEL ........ 41

7. Travel Didn't Go As Planned ........ 42

8. Lesson Learned from a Mule ........ 49

9. Injured in the Middle of Nowhere ........ 54

10. Extreme Emotions at Airports ........ 60

11. How God Used a Vanity License Plate ........ 67

12.  Deadly Detour: Following the Wrong Leader     71

SECTION III: GOD'S PROVIDENCE IN MY CHILDHOOD     77

13.  The Impact of the Family Boss     78

14.  Mama's Desperate Christmas Eve     86

15.  Doctor's Prediction I'd Go Insane     90

16.  When the FBI Came to Our Home     98

17.  Letting Go of My Treasures     102

18.  Reaction to a Hate Prank     107

19.  From Abandoned Daughter to Found Fiancée     110

PHOTOS     118

SECTION IV:  GOD'S PLAN IN MY SPIRITUAL FORMATION     125

20.  Childhood Threads Woven for God's Purposes     126

21.  A Longing to Belong     132

22.  When Rose-colored Glasses Were a Good Thing     136

SECTION V: GOD'S PRESENCE IN MY CHILDREN'S LIVES     143

23.  House Arrest with Our Baby     144

24.  A School Choice Dilemma     148

25.  When Our Kids' Valuables Were Stolen     155

26.  A Treasure Born in a Village     159

27.  Jeered by the Spectators     168

28.  A Grandfather's Act of Mercy     174

29.  Adoption: Blocked                                       182

SECTION VI: GOD'S PURPOSE SEEN IN LIFE                      187
AND DEATH

30.  Runaway Dad is Located                                 188

31.  Bad Advice Disguised as Caution                        196

32.  God Said No When I Needed a Yes                        202

33.  Hurting People Hurt People                             208

34.  When God Appointed a Deer                              211

35.  Assignment: Steadfastness                              216

FINAL WORDS                                                 221

ENDNOTES                                                    223

ACKNOWLEDGEMENTS                                            229

ABOUT THE AUTHOR                                            231

A LETTER TO THE READER                                      233

# PREFACE: An Invitation to Change Worry to Wonder

THE YOUNG NURSE INSERTED a needle into my neck. She was drawing another biopsy sample from one of my six thyroid nodules.

A neck ultrasound to check my carotid arteries had revealed abnormal nodules. I had noticed that I was sometimes hoarse, which can be a symptom of thyroid cancer.

I wondered how God planned to bring good from this possible diagnosis.

I smiled at the nurse as I told her about the goodness of God in my life. She listened politely, but her forehead was wrinkled with confusion. I wondered if she was thinking, "Aren't you worried?"

Actually, no. No, I was not worried, although the temptation is always there. God is sovereign in my life, and everything that happens to me is filtered through His loving hands. And I trust Him.

But it wasn't always like this for me.

Memories of trauma from our time in Ethiopia and Ghana, as well as from my childhood and my kids' experiences, are harsh realities. Some of the most vivid ones were:

- That time we ran low on food. What if I gave away most of our pantry items? Would God provide for our family until we could shop?

- How fearful I was when we missed our train in a foreign country that had a curfew. Where would we find safety until morning?

- The desertion of my dad and the impact it had on my family. Without income, how would we survive?

- Wanting to protect my children from bad things happening to them. But was I the one in charge?

The list of my worry opportunities went on and on. However, as I reflected on them, I could see how God brought good from every single one. In some cases, the "good" He brought about was a lesson He taught me from it. I smiled at the wonder of God's goodness.

And then it hit me right there on that examination table: I needed to write a book about how God changed my worry to wonder!

You are now reading that book. I invite you to experience these trials in my life with me: Worrisome. Anxious. Nail-biting trials.

And then wonder with me at God's goodness as I reflect on them in life's rearview mirror.

These stories are not presented chronologically but instead are grouped thematically. I have included the date and location at the beginning of each story to help orient you. Check the *ENDNOTES* chapter for more information.

Whether or not I can see how God brought good from one of my trials is not the measuring stick of His goodness. Occasionally, I still can't see it in some of what He allowed in my life other than the lessons He taught me. But I trust Him and believe He did (and continues to) bring good from everything He allowed (and allows) in my life.

I still am tempted to worry when presented with a trial, but I am asking God to help me remain steadfast quicker than ever. I want to shift from worrying as my default attitude to embracing the wonder of God before I know what He will do.

My goals for you are twofold:

1. You, too, will reflect on the worrisome trials God has allowed in your life and see how God brought good from them.

2. You will learn to trust God in your current trial to bring good out of it before seeing His marvelous plan.

I invite you to change your worry opportunities into worship opportunities at the wonder of God's goodness.

Oh, one more thing: my thyroid biopsies were all benign. For now, anyway.

Living in the wonder of God's goodness to me,
Amy Hagerup
Dousman, Wisconsin

A note on names and specific details in this memoir:

I have used most of the family and friends' real names (with permission) in these stories. I have changed the names of a few minor roles. Everything is as accurate as I can remember. But as you and I know, memories evolve and grow as we do. The resounding message remains true despite a non-perfect memory: God is at work in our trials and works them all together for good to those who love Him (Romans 8:28).

Unless noted otherwise, all Scripture verses are quoted in the English Standard Version.

# God's Provision of Every Need

# Assignment: Loneliness

**May 1975 ~ Ethiopia**

Staring out the 747's window at the mountains, I saw circles of huts huddled together like a football team before a play. *I'm back.*

I had spent a summer in Ethiopia as a short-term missionary with the Sudan Interior Mission, known simply as SIM. (The mission name was changed later, but the acronym remained the same.)

My fiancé and I had flown in together a year ago. Mark had then started his first four-year term by traveling south to Soddo while I served for three months in the pharmacy in Addis Ababa. Even though we were not together during my stint there, it was a valuable time to learn the culture and get to know Ethiopians working at the headquarters. As a twenty-one-year-old who had seldom been out of South Carolina, my worldview was expanded by making friendships with colleagues from other countries: Scotland, Germany, Australia, Canada, and Ireland. I had much to learn.

At the end of the summer, I had flown back to the United States to complete my final year of Bible college. During those eight months at home, I had finished my senior year, written my doctrinal thesis for college and my mission board, packed my barrels, and raised support.

Since we hoped to start a family during our first term overseas, I gathered maternity clothes and baby items to pack. One time, when I was shopping for a maternity dress, the sales lady asked me when my baby was due. "In about two years," I said. I don't know if that was presumption or faith on my part, but they did get used in Ethiopia.

My final preparation step for returning to the mission field was to fly to SIM's three-week candidate school in New Jersey. I packed my wedding dress in my carry-on bag. After I completed candidate school, I flew to Ethiopia to join Mark and begin our married life.

I was landing in this beautiful country where God was planting me.

I would see Mark soon.

And I couldn't stop smiling!

Ten days after arriving, Mark and I recited our vows in a garden behind the mission headquarters in Addis Ababa. I was sorry that none of our families were able to attend our special occasion. But we had to decide whether to get married in Ethiopia after I graduated or wait three more years for us to return to the U.S. on our first furlough. We chose the earliest wedding date possible.

After our honeymoon at the mission's retreat location and a life-defining trip to Djibouti, Mark and I started language study in Debre Berhan. Mark had already learned some Amharic, so he was in the second-year class. I was in the beginning class.

During those early months of language school, I started feeling tired and needed to nap daily. It didn't take long to realize the exciting news—those maternity clothes would be required! We sent the news in an aerogram to my sister with the instruction to take a photo of my mother when she found out she would be a grandmother.

That is still one of my favorite photos: Anna reading the news out loud while my brother captured the moment of Mama clapping and jumping.

My severe morning sickness put a damper on my language study, especially the essential visitation we did daily. However, I completed the first year of study with flying colors as well as an expanding girth. Mark finished the advanced level. We were on our way.

In January 1976, after finishing language school, we were stationed at Soddo, where Mark had been while I was finishing college. The mission compound included a hospital and a row of missionary houses where doctors, nurses, and teaching missionaries lived. On February 9, I gave birth to Benjamin Mark in that hospital.

The missionaries became our family, and we devoured meals and games together on Friday nights. Since Mark and I were in our early twenties, we were closer in age to the high school missionary kids than we were to our fellow career missionaries. But the seasoned missionaries became our close friends—and four of the nurses joined us in Ghana years later.

One weekend, a young SIM family came for a visit to Soddo. We met them during the game night that Friday. They ministered in Waka, which was only accessible by pack mule or Mission Aviation Fellowship aircraft. (MAF is a missions organization that provides flights to missionaries in remote locations.) Simon and Jenna Harmon and their three small children joined us for a meal. With brown hair framing her face, Jenna punctuated her stories with hand gestures. Her reports fascinated me; their life was much more isolated than ours in Soddo.

The tone of our conversation changed when she leaned close to my face and whispered, "Amy, pray that you never get assigned to Waka. You will die of loneliness there." I watched her eyes glaze over, and I instinctively hugged her.

About four weeks later, our mission head, Merle, knocked on our screen door. "Anyone home?" His eyes showed seriousness as he sat on our new purple couch, which we had ordered built from a carpenter in Soddo. We had spent $150 of our $200 monthly income on this sofa, which was the second piece of furniture we had made. The first one was a blue-and-white crib for Benjy.

I brought Merle a cup of tea and then took Benjy onto my lap as I sat down beside Mark.

"Mark and Amy, the Harmons you met last month are leaving the mission field. I want you to pray about moving to Waka to replace them. I normally would not ask a new missionary couple to go to a hardship post, but I have no alternative." He laced his fingers together as he leaned forward.

I froze in my chair as Jenna's warning echoed in my brain. Mark blinked as he absorbed this request. Everything seemed to move in slow motion. Even the curtains stopped fluttering.

Merle was waiting for a response.

"Of course, we will pray about this." My husband glanced at me for my support. I nodded, thinking of how we had just settled into our third home in Soddo—a cute little cottage without bats (unlike the other two we had lived in). A move to Waka would mean leaving behind both our purple couch and the blue-and-white crib. But the loss of these purchases didn't compare to the terrifying possibility of what awaited me there.

One life-robbing word consumed my thoughts: loneliness.

Refusing to move to Waka was not an option. God had led us through every assignment of our short married lives and continued to guide us. We knew the best place to be was in the center of His will. He didn't make mistakes. *But Waka?*

One month later, in August 1976, we moved to Waka with our six-month-old son.

Waka was a two-day mule ride from Soddo or a thirty-minute flight. SIM equipped the missionary houses in remote stations so furniture didn't have to be flown in and out every time a missionary changed. All we had to bring was our clothing and home supplies like pots and pans, linens, and other personal effects. The couch our mission provided was a chocolate-colored tweed, and Benjy's crib was a walnut stain. Each piece of furniture performed its purposes splendidly. Everything in our little cottage was a generous provision in the middle of these mountains.

My husband's roles in our new location were teaching in the Bible school and preaching in outlying villages. The church was well-established, so our involvement was more in teaching and encouraging the church than church planting. For Mark, this involved trekking for several days into the mountains to reach fledgling churches and teach them God's Word. He would do this with Ethiopian church leaders who had helped establish the churches years earlier. It was a privilege for us to be working alongside such godly men.

I enjoyed teaching the Bible to ladies and teenage girls each week. My Amharic improved as I used it in visiting and teaching. Mark and I also worked on memorizing verses to grow our vocabulary in our newly-acquired language.

We ran a generator some nights for an hour but used it sparingly since we had to fly in the diesel fuel to operate it. A wood stove was used to boil our drinking water, bake bread, and cook our meals; it had the added benefit of heating our home. A gas stove was available for occasional cooking when we didn't have the wood stove cranked up. Our "refrigerator" was a unique screened window that protruded, complete with shelves and an interior wooden door to cover it. Temperatures were cool in the mountains, especially in the evenings. In that makeshift cooler, we could store a small jar of mayonnaise purchased in Addis Ababa and finish it before it went bad.

Our tub was old-fashioned with feet. When we got into it, we had to be sure we stepped into the middle because it would rock precariously. Our water supply came down the hill through a buried garden hose to our kitchen sink and the rocking tub. It was only a bit more than a trickle, but we were thankful for it. And for our toilet, we had an outhouse.

Once we were unpacked in Waka and the novelty wore off, loneliness did rear its ugliness in my heart. I was a new mother in a foreign country with difficult living circumstances. I had no other female to share my heart. My husband was my best friend in every way, and after struggling with an absent father in my childhood, Mark was a dream come true. He loved and cherished me and was a great dad to our son.

But I needed a girlfriend to chat with. At least that lie took hold in my heart as I succumbed to a "poor me" attitude.

Mark sympathized with my loneliness; he hated to see me feeling down. He directed me to God's truths, but I continued to be discontent. I figured he couldn't understand what I was going through; he thrived on his treks into remote villages while I stayed home.

After a while, Mark said, "Amy, go out and visit someone. The answer to your loneliness is in your power." Even though his voice was not harsh—just tender compassion for his hurting wife—I was annoyed by his suggestion. *What does he know about how hard this is for me?*

But God used his words to jolt me to action.

Pulling myself together and asking God for strength, I decided to visit someone. With Benjy on my back and my Bible in my hand, I trekked up the dirt path through the middle of our village. I walked past the tin-roofed school building on my left, waving to the students. At the top of the hill, I branched off to a hut on the side of the mountain, where I knew of a young woman about my age who lived with her husband and baby.

Ribkah, with her baby on her hip, squealed with delight when she saw Benjy and me. She pulled a low stool beside her, and I obligingly sat on it. I put Benjy on the ground near her young son.

The two little boys began to play with a few spoons Ribkah gave them. I stumbled with my Amharic and improvised with gestures and smiles. We laughed together as we nibbled on *kolo* (roasted corn) and watched our babies play. In those moments, I forgot about my limited Amharic and majored in the language of friendliness.

I shared verses from my Amharic Bible with her. She leaned forward and followed the lines as I read, repeating some keywords. The fire was dying out, but I felt warm inside.

Sitting there contemplating Ribkah's everyday life, I gained a new perspective. My eyes were opened to her needs and how I could be a friend to her.

I had a preconceived idea of how I wanted God to answer my loneliness prayer: give me a friend like me—someone from the same culture and a similar situation in life. Then I wouldn't be lonely.

But that wasn't true at all. God wanted to enrich my life by having me reach out to someone different from me to whom I could show love. A world of needy people was right outside my door. It was up to me to find them.

Being a missionary wasn't only about sharing the gospel and teaching Bible studies. It was about living life together—chatting around an open fire while little ones played, walking, shopping in the market, and eating *kolo* together. It was about being honest with each other—hurting parts included.

I had a choice: I could wrap myself in my distress and die a little bit more each day in my loneliness. Or I could realize that God had a reason for where He had placed me and what I was experiencing. I could shift my focus from solving my pain to reaching out to encourage others in their life challenges.

My loneliness had a purpose, but I had to open my eyes to it and obey His promptings.

That afternoon, I retraced the path home with a new spring in my step.

I remembered Ribkah waving goodbye. Perhaps she thought, "I don't feel so lonely anymore."

And I couldn't stop smiling.

Philippians 2:3: Do nothing from selfish ambition or conceit, but in humility count others more significant than yourselves.

# Chapter Two

# Down to My Last Two Dollars

**Fall 1969 ~ Columbia, South Carolina**

TEARS CAME TO MY eyes when the presentation showed wide-eyed children huddled around the missionary with an open Bible on her lap. I leaned forward in the pew to hear every word about spreading the gospel overseas. I was only sixteen, but I could already imagine my future mission involvement.

Even though August Street Church had fewer than one hundred members, it was focused on missions. I savored hearing the missionaries from around the world share their stories. If the speaker had a ministry in China, then I also wanted to minister in China. If the speaker served the Lord in Peru, then Peru was where I wanted to serve. The missionaries sharing that day were from Nigeria. *Maybe I'll go to Africa.*

As was my church's custom during the conference, everyone was asked to pray about how much money they would commit to giving for the following year. I earned about twenty dollars a week babysitting, so I pledged to give two dollars every Sunday for missions.

I used my babysitting income for my lunch money and different personal needs. Since my dad had deserted our family when I was ten, I wanted to assist my mom as much as possible—sometimes buying milk or gas with my earnings. I saved a portion, too.

The year progressed, and I gave two dollars for missions every week.

But one Sunday, when the offering plate was about to be passed, I opened my wallet and saw that I had only two dollars. I searched my inside pockets for a secret stash. Nothing. Just two measly green bills with George Washington staring back at me.

My mind went into overdrive. I had no babysitting jobs lined up that week, not even on Friday or Saturday nights. The families who booked me most frequently would schedule me weeks or sometimes months in advance, but I had no job for the week before me.

I twisted my watch nervously as I considered the worst-case scenario. *If I give my last two dollars, I will have no lunch money for tomorrow, let alone the rest of the week.*

❧ ⤜⤜

When we moved to Columbia in June 1966 after my dad deserted us, I spent that summer without a single friend. I was recovering from the sudden separation from my childhood best friend, Charlotte, whom I left in Georgia. So I decided to offer babysitting services to our neighbors. I made a flier announcing a new local babysitter, giving a few references and providing my contact information. My mother drove me around our subdivision to distribute the fliers. I put one into mailboxes at homes where I saw evidence of children: tricycle in the carport, crib bars seen through the windows, a Pampers box sticking out of the garbage can. That very night, I got a call for my first job.

And so my babysitting business began. I collected new neighbors' names and phone numbers like most normal thirteen-year-old girls collected fingernail polish. From eighth through twelfth grades, I was more interested in babysitting than dating, although I did attend football games with friends if I didn't have a job that night.

God used children to fill my life and heart. As I walked up the hill on Luster Lane one evening to a red brick house, I could see two-year-old Jill with her nose pressed against the screen door. Catching sight of me, she squealed, "Mamie is here! Mamie is here!" I lifted and swung her around on the fake-brick kitchen floor. I loved these kids as much as they loved me.

Mrs. Burris called in early November to ask me to babysit on New Year's Eve. When she learned I was already booked, she asked me to reserve New Year's Eve for the following year. The Nickases on Morninghill Drive would book me for all the Gamecocks' home football games as soon as the schedule came out. Now that was job security.

During the school year, I could only work at night and on the weekends. My average weekly earnings of about twenty dollars was impressive, considering my pay was only fifty cents per hour (seventy-five cents after midnight).

Along with my devotion to children, I followed in my mother's footsteps to know and love Jesus. All my employers knew I wasn't available on Sunday mornings; church attendance was non-negotiable.

One Sunday, as I opened the bulletin, I saw that the next missions conference was coming up in October. I eagerly read over the bio of the missionary who would be sharing with us. Dr. Titus Payne was an ophthalmologist who used his skills as an inroad to share the gospel in Nigeria with SIM.

I couldn't wait for October to get here.

My fingers reached for the two bills that were avoiding being caught.

I required supernatural assistance to pull out those bills and place them in the offering plate. As I put them on the maroon velvet,

I asked God to provide what I would need during the upcoming week, particularly for lunch the next day. Seeing what God would do would be fascinating, but I admit I was nervous about it.

When we got home after church, I stepped on the cement stair in our carport and opened the back door. The beige phone hanging on the wall in the kitchen rang impatiently. A neighbor needed me to babysit that afternoon. *Hello, lunch money for Monday!*

A couple hours later, someone else called and wanted me to babysit that night. Then someone called, asking me to babysit on Monday night.

I continued to get calls throughout the week: I had one or two babysitting jobs every day that week, and three on Saturday.

That week, I made a record-breaking seventy-five dollars!

God abundantly provided after I gave my last two dollars. I felt like an Israelite during their Exodus wanderings when they woke up that first morning to see abundant food on the ground: a mixture of surprise, awe, thankfulness, and reverence.

Lunch on Monday seemed like manna from heaven. And indeed it was.

Malachi 3:10 (NASB): "Bring the whole tithe into the storehouse . . . and test Me now in this," says the Lord of hosts, "if I will not open for you the windows of heaven and pour out for you a blessing until it overflows."

# Chapter Three

# A Needed Item I Forgot to Bring

**Summer 1978 ~ Palatine, Illinois**

WHEN PACKING FOR OUR first four-year missionary term in Ghana, I felt pressure not to forget anything significant. To buy everything needed to set up our household overseas was a daunting task. Lists filled my spiral notebook.

With two children under two years of age and another baby on the way, we were taking our young family to West Africa for a four-year term.

I made a chart of the children's ages on each birthday and Christmas for the four years we would be there. That way, I could plan presents for them for each event. To make my preparation more challenging, we didn't know the gender of our third child, who would be born after we got there. I had to plan gender-neutral gifts for child number three.

Packing the barrels was a drawn-out process. Many items had to be carefully considered and packed. I had purchased two saucepans: a two-quart and a three-quart. Their silver lids sported a narrow black handle, making them easier to lift when cooking. I nestled the pots in the barrel of kitchen items and padded them with sunflower dish towels. I gave them a final pat as if putting them to bed for the long trip by boat across the Atlantic Ocean.

I've always loved things that matched.

When we lived in the remote village of Waka in Ethiopia with our first baby, I used red gingham cloth to make curtains for his nursery windows. Then, I sewed a gingham skirt to hang around a big barrel for the changing table. I used solid red material to cover pieces of cardboard to make mats for teddy bear photos from an old calendar. They looked adorable, hanging on the wall above Benjy's crib. As rustic and homemade as it was, my baby's room matched, and I adored it.

Once, I sewed a jumper for myself, then used the leftover plaid cloth to sew a romper for Benjy. We matched. It was one of the quirks God put in me: I felt a deep contentment when things matched.

So, our barrels and crates would cross the ocean to join us in Ghana. Once they arrived, I could set up my kitchen—matching pots and all.

December 1978

Kumasi, Ghana

The thrilling day came when a massive truck arrived in our yard in Kumasi with our crates and barrels from America. We had been in Ghana for three months. Our nearby missionary colleagues had loaned us the essentials to set up the house until our supplies arrived. Today felt like Christmas.

Everything was offloaded. The heavy barrels were rolled into our garage, where we could open them over the following weeks. It would be delightful to set up my kitchen with my matching items.

Mark unlocked the padlocks on each barrel and pried off two lids. Benjy, almost three years old, held his arms up for any treasure I would give him to carry into the house. As I handed him a blue bath towel, he hugged it to his face, declaring its softness as he took it inside. I could only get a barrel about halfway unpacked by myself. Being close to delivering baby number three, my protruding belly was not conducive to barrel diving. But I pressed on.

I had kept a record of what was in each barrel, so I knew my kitchen items were in barrel number eight. There they were: my two matching saucepans tucked in snugly by dish towels. I gingerly pulled them out even though they were far from breakable. In sheer joy, I hugged them to my chest, then glanced around to see if Mark had witnessed my frivolity. *Safe!*

My kitchen's cupboards proudly displayed the pots on their designated shelves. A sunflower dishtowel was draped over the oven handle; yellow curtains hung limply in the heat of Kumasi. What a darling kitchen. Everything matched.

A few weeks later, I realized I had a problem: my two saucepans were too large for certain cooking needs. *Why didn't I splurge and purchase some smaller sizes?* I had thought bigger would better suit our growing family. After all, who cooks rice in a one-quart saucepan?

I pulled the two-quart pot out of the cupboard. I couldn't believe this was the smallest one I had brought for a four-year term in Ghana. *What was I thinking?*

In my naivety, I had thought that a two-quart saucepan, a three-quart saucepan, a frying pan, and a pressure cooker would meet all my cooking needs for our family of five. But boiling some eggs or making a child-size serving of oatmeal was nearly impossible without a smaller pot.

Blond-haired Benjy tugged on my dress. "Mommy, can you make some Jell-O?" *I could if I had a pot that was small enough. Oh well, I can make do. This is a small problem in God's economy.*

I made the Jell-O.

Christmas 1979

When our second Christmas rolled around, I chose the children's gifts from the storage barrel—gifts I had purchased in America. Benjy was receiving some large cardboard building blocks we would assemble on Christmas Eve. Deeanne was getting a baby doll and miniature stroller. Almost-one-year-old Heidi was getting colorful pop beads and stacking donuts to chew on to her heart's content. She was still at the stage of exploring her environment by tasting it.

My shivers of anticipation for Christmas morning made it hard to sleep that night. I knew these were gifts they would treasure. Delighting one's children with surprises is a satisfying feeling.

Christmas dawned with the anticipation of the day vibrating through our home. We centered the celebration on Jesus' birth, and the joy of receiving gifts was an added privilege. I beamed like the sun as I watched our children's exuberance—Benjy in his yellow pajamas and the girls in their matching blue nightgowns. I'm not sure who was blessed more: the giver or the recipients. *Probably the giver!*

Once the new year rolled in, we made a trip to Accra and visited some missionary friends who we knew from our church in Illinois. Fellowshipping with other missionaries was always a highlight; the ones who had children our kids' ages were extra special. We laughed and shared stories around the dinner table, scraping our bowls to get the last taste of tangy groundnut stew. The children went off to play while Donna and I cleared the table. Heidi, who couldn't walk yet, played on the floor.

Carrying a large pot to the kitchen, I told the hostess about my disappointment when I realized I had failed to bring small saucepans in our barrels. I sighed and said, "I have two-quart and three-quart saucepans, but nothing smaller. I don't know what I was thinking."

Donna's eyes lit up. "Oh, Amy, I have two little ones I never use. They are pushed to the back of the cabinet. You can have them."

I followed her to her cupboards like an eager puppy about to get a treat. I never realized I could get so worked up anticipating the gift of two saucepans.

She pulled out her frequently used pots and set them on the cement floor. Then she reached back into the bottom shelf and pulled out a one-quart saucepan, followed by a one-and-a-half-quart size along with their lids.

As soon as they came into my view, I gasped. I couldn't believe what I was seeing. The narrow black handle was right down the middle of the lid—exactly like mine in Kumasi. They matched my other two saucepans!

God is such a fantastic gift giver. He enjoys giving us good gifts and loves to see His children delighted.

Was it essential that these two pots matched my set? Of course not!

But God knew I would like that. He made me to be like that.

In His sovereignty, however my friend came in possession of these pots, God had them be the same ones that would match my set. He was planning to get them to me—His precious daughter who He knew loved for things to match.

While hugging her, I said, "Thank you so much, Donna."

She whispered, "Oh, Amy. I was just the conduit. God planned them for you all along."

Matthew 7:11 (NASB): If you then, being evil, know how to give good gifts to your children, how much more will your Father who is in heaven give what is good to those who ask Him!

# Chapter Four

# A Powerful Lesson from God's Provision

**May 1982 ~ Furlough, U.S.**

ANTICIPATING A ONE-YEAR FURLOUGH was intoxicating, especially after a four-year term in Africa. The thrill of international flights and brief sightseeing in Europe (Amsterdam this time) during our trip home was exciting. Then, once we transitioned to American life, we would experience the luxury of washing dishes with hot water right from the tap, indulging in yummy food, and, best of all, reuniting with family and friends.

However, the reality of planning for furlough was stressful: we wondered how God would provide for our living needs, especially housing and transportation. On our first furlough, we divided our time equally between my home in South Carolina and Mark's home in Illinois. But now that our older children were school-age, we had to settle in one area for the academic year. Also, the majority of our support came from churches in the Midwest. Although I knew I would miss my family while we were based in the Chicago area, I knew I would get to see them several times during our furlough.

Our own little family had grown since our last time in the U.S. We had left in 1978 with a two-year-old and an eight-month-old; now we were returning with three children ages six, four, and three. Staying with Mark's parents would not work for more than a week or so. Renting a house for a family of five on a missionary income was almost unheard of in the Chicago suburbs. We needed transportation, too, but couldn't negotiate from Africa for it. During our family devotions, we prayed for these needs. How would God answer? And when?

I started reading from our stack of mail when I reached a letter from our faithful supporters from Arlington Heights, the LaRues. I shouted to Mark: "Good news! The LaRues say they have a house near your folks we can use for our furlough!" God had provided a furnished home from supporters who were leaving for a one-year work assignment in Arizona. Their home was near both our home church and an elementary school.

A week later, the "good-news-from-home" scenario repeated itself. Mark handed his parents' blue aerogram letter to me with a grin on his face. "More good news," he said. Mark's parents had purchased a blue Pacer from their niece for our use. There was our provision for transportation. God continued in His faithfulness to provide everything we needed. *Why did I ever worry?*

Furlough flew by. God provided positive school experiences for second-grade Benjy and kindergartener Deeanne at Patton Elementary School. We reveled in deep connections at our supporting churches, filling our emotional buckets. We were provided free dental and doctor appointments at one missions conference. Friends surprised us with groceries and invited our children for playdates. God was pulling out all the stops to provide for our physical and emotional needs before we headed back to the rigors of the mission field.

We purchased the supplies we needed for our next term and packed crates again—fewer than last time. Mark's folks let us use their garage for our packing headquarters. They were always generous with us.

Before we knew it, April 1983 arrived. We cleaned out the LaRues' home and moved in with Mark's parents, Mom and Dad Hagerup, for our last five days in Illinois. We would fly to Columbia to see my extended family before flying to Ghana.

⤜⤜⤜   ⤛⤛⤛

The plastic airport chairs were stiff and could have been more accommodating as Heidi squeezed beside me. "Delta Flight 356 is now boarding to Columbia, South Carolina. Those traveling with young children may now board."

We exchanged long embraces with Mark's parents as we said goodbye at O'Hare airport for our next two-and-a-half-year term. Mark handed the Pacer's keys to his dad and thanked him again. That compact blue car had served us well.

The five of us walked down the Jetway to the Boeing 757. The children skipped in excitement, each holding a small carry-on. I smiled at their antics while thinking about the significance of walking this Jetway. It was like a transition tunnel for us—from one assignment in life to the next. *How many Jetways have we walked already?*

The flight attendant's voice shook me out of my reverie. "Well, hello," she said to five-year-old Deeanne. "Is this your first flight?" I had to chuckle as I heard my middle child's innocent response. That lady had no idea she was talking to a miniature world traveler.

We settled into our three blue seats while Mark and Benjy climbed into theirs across the aisle. I buckled my daughters' seat belts as they craned their necks to survey the activity outside the oval window. Our flight from Chicago was departing soon.

We would be in Columbia with my family and our South Carolina supporting church for the next two weeks. I was a bubbling pot of joy to know I would be reunited with Mama and my siblings in a few hours.

Mama had told me of some of the plans for our time in Columbia. Aunt Anna Tompkins wanted to take us to the zoo after Sunday dinner, which would include her famous yeast rolls. My older sister was hosting a cookout. I had a dentist's appointment on Thursday. Last-minute shopping was always a given right before leaving the country.

But there was one problem: we no longer had the Pacer and would need a car to get around for these errands. My mother would have gladly given us her vehicle to use, but she needed it to drive to the high school where she taught.

I'm the type of person who likes to plan—to know what is happening and how our needs will be met. God had graciously revealed our housing and transportation for our time in Illinois before we left Ghana. But I had no clue how God would provide us with a vehicle these last weeks. Thinking about it was like a storm cloud hovering over my head. The time was getting short, and we still didn't know how we would be able to get to our appointments. Sometimes, I mistakenly thought I should help God with the answer, but there was nothing I could do. I needed to trust God for the sun to break through the dark clouds.

Our family of five crowded into my mother's Dodge Coronet on Sunday as we headed to church. Arriving in the parking lot, we were met by friends who poured abundant hugs on us. I drank in each one as my emotional tank filled up more.

Augusta Street Church claims an esteemed place in my heart. God used this body of believers during my teenage years to point me toward missions. They had committed to a substantial part of our monthly support from the beginning of our missionary career.

Pastor Von Nessen welcomed us during the service and shared our need for a vehicle to borrow for the next two weeks. Sitting at the piano, my mother was a beaming ray of sunshine, thrilled that her missionary children and grandchildren were in the service.

After everyone had finished singing the closing song, church members Rob and Barri approached our pew as we stood. They told us they had purchased a new Volkswagen van, but they still had their old van, which they planned to sell. Rob said, "It will be no problem for us to hold off selling it so we can loan you a van for two weeks." And just like that, the sun broke through the clouds! Our faithful God had answered once again.

*What an excellent provision! Not just a sedan but a van.*

That afternoon, they drove both vans to Mama's home, where we were staying. We chatted in the yard, and then Rob handed my husband the keys to the *new* van.

I reacted quickly: "Oh no, Rob. We don't want to drive your new van. We want to use the old one. The old one is all we need."

Rob didn't miss a beat as Barri's coy smile awaited his response.

"Amy, we are not giving the van to *you*. We are giving it to *Jesus*. And we want to give Him our *best*!"

Exodus 23:19: The best of the first fruits of your ground you shall bring into the house of the Lord your God.

# Chapter Five

# No One Can Outgive God!

## August 1985 ~ Kumasi, Ghana

WHEN WE RETURNED FROM our four-month furlough with our kids, now nine, seven, and six, and drove into our yard in Kumasi, everything looked the same until our friends came out to greet us. They had obviously lost weight.

The drought of 1983–84 had caused a severe food shortage and starvation. Mark had been involved in famine relief with grain distribution. Early rains had come this year, so local crops would become available soon.

On our drive home from Accra, we stopped for lunch at a chop bar (a small roadside food stand). Yams and plantain were still available. These tubers were used to make the national dish, *fufu*, served with soup and small pieces of meat. Fufu was a treat for us and the kids.

We didn't want to buy fresh fruit being sold on the side of the road because we knew that those selling it probably needed it more than we did. We were thankful for our yard's mango, avocado, and papaya trees so we could enjoy eating and sharing the fruit when it was in season.

We unloaded our suitcases and boxes from the truck and began unpacking. I had marked one of the storage barrels: "Open me first." It contained bed sheets, towels, toilet paper, basic pots, dishes, and a few canned goods. Our food supply was low, but we would travel to the neighboring country of Togo to buy more soon.

After the roller coaster family goodbyes and international flights, being back home again in Kumasi felt like a peaceful oasis.

A couple evenings later, an elderly couple seeking food knocked on our door. Nine-year-old Benjy answered and called me to come. I introduced myself to them and began chatting. Kwame seemed weaker than his wife, Abenaa. My heart ached for them as I realized their desperation to come to me—a stranger. I told them to wait while I went to our pantry.

These visitors' plight impacted me deeply. Perhaps it was a result of arriving from America the previous week. The memory of grocery stores having entire aisles of dry cereal was fresh. I remember one time during family devotions, Mark taught about the exodus of the children of Israel. When he asked our kids what they knew about the promised land, Benjy said, "It's just like America—full of milk and honey!"

Benjy followed me and watched as I pushed aside the bottles of ketchup and vinegar, searching for what could be consumed as a meal. I only had four cans of mackerel, a two-pound bag of rice, and some eggs in the refrigerator.

I tried to fight off the feeling that if I gave this away, I might not have enough for what we needed. Childhood memories of empty cupboards fed that feeling. However, remembering God's faithful provision also peppered my recall. In instances like this begging couple, I had a choice of which feeling to act on: the worry of my family having enough or the wonder of how God would provide.

Thankfully, I chose the latter. I decided to give half of everything we had, trusting the Lord to supply our needs until we could travel to Togo.

"Let's pack up some eggs for them, too, Benjy," I said as I bagged up the rice and cans of mackerel. He ran to his bedroom and grabbed some of his *cedis* (Ghanaian currency, pronounced see-dees) to include with what I was giving them. "Here, Mommy, add this." His eyes sparkled as he thrust a few bills into the plastic bag. Witnessing my son's response to the Spirit working in his young heart warmed mine.

After I shared the provisions, I sat beside Kwame and Abenaa to offer something much better than these few food items. I told them about Jesus being the Living Bread and how He had come to earth to save us from our sins.

I read Romans 3:23, explaining that we are all sinners and fall short of God's perfect standard. Then, I turned to Romans 6:23: "The wages of sin is death, but the free gift of God is eternal life in Christ Jesus our Lord." John 1:12 summed up what they needed to do: "But to all who did receive him, who believed in his name, he gave the right to become children of God."

I communicated with them in my rusty Twi. The Holy Spirit filled in the gaps and opened their spiritual eyes. They both accepted the Lord Jesus into their lives that night.

The joy I felt of a new sister and brother in the Lord far outweighed my wondering how our family would get enough food over the next few weeks.

⇝⇝ ⇜⇜

The next day, some missionary friends drove into our yard. Our whole family ran outside as the Hansons' pickup truck doors slammed behind them. They welcomed us back with bear hugs while the five kids (three of ours and two of theirs) darted into the house. Jeanette was carrying a big basket, and I saw canned goods peeking out with a loaf of bread perched on top. She said, "We know you haven't been able to get to Togo yet, so we brought some food to help you out." *Great timing!*

Living in Kumasi made us a good stopping point for missionaries traveling between Accra (four hours' drive south of us) and Tamale (seven hours drive to the north). The same day the Hansons brought that basket of food, a fellow missionary, Mark Lundstedt, stopped by to overnight with us on his way to Accra.

Mark L. brought us half a sack of powdered milk. He handed my Mark the heavy bag. "I know you are just back from furlough and haven't been able to go to Togo yet, so Tedde and I thought we would share our milk powder with you." *Amazing!*

Our pantry was getting restocked.

But God wasn't finished yet.

A young Southern Baptist missionary couple stopped by our home the next day. "Hey Hagerups. Welcome back to Ghana. How was your furlough?" They were carrying two bulging grocery bags.

Lori set the bag on our dining room table and said, "We were cleaning out our pantry before we leave for furlough. We thought you could use some foodstuffs since you haven't been able to go to Togo yet." Inside the bags were canned food items from America, including a ham.

God provided all our needs in abundance—even a ham from America.

Benjy joined me in the pantry as I put the last can on the shelf. "God did this, didn't He, Mommy?"

"Yes, son, He did."

And I thought, *No one can outgive God!*

About a week later, we arrived home from one of the villages and found Abenaa, the elderly woman we had gifted with half our pantry items, on our back steps. Her head was bowed, buried in her hands, and she seemed to be crying.

I got out of the car and went to sit beside her. My stomach twisted into a knot as I felt her sadness and immediately knew the cause: her husband Kwame, who had been sick for several months, had died.

I held her for a while, letting my embrace and tears communicate to her spirit that I hurt with her. I shared the hope of glory and the joy of knowing her husband was out of misery and with our living God. First John 5:13 says, "I write these things to you who believe in the name of the Son of God, that you may know that you have eternal life."

Her serene expression and nod told me she understood. We would see Kwame again someday.

With my arm around her thin shoulders, I rested my cheek on the top of her headscarf, smelling the fragrance of her hair oils. I closed my eyes and imagined her husband, who had sat in this exact spot a mere week ago, now in Jesus' arms.

The night they came, I had given them a gift of food. It was a gift—no payment was needed because we had already purchased it. The food was ours to give. All they had to do was receive it, which they did.

And then I offered them the gift of eternal life through believing in Jesus. It also was a gift—Jesus had already paid for it. All they had to do was receive it, which they did.

I was able to share some imperfect food to sustain physical life briefly.

But God was able to give perfect spiritual food for eternal life with Him. And no human can do that.

Indeed, no human can outgive God's gift of salvation.

James 1:17: Every good gift and every perfect gift is from above, coming down from the Father of lights, with whom there is no variation or shadow due to change.

# Chapter Six

# Too Exhausted to Serve a Visitor

**January 1988 ~ Kumasi, Ghana**

Pinching the final clothespin, I pulled Mark's blue-striped shirt off the clothesline and placed it in the basket. I wiped my brow.

Tiredness permeated my body. Washing clothes in the United States involved the simple turn of a knob that resulted in clothes being put through the cycle of washing, rinsing, and spinning. In Ghana, I had a washing machine made from half of a barrel—designed and created by my brilliant brother-in-law, Scott. Agitating the clothes involved me swinging a paddle back and forth along the bottom of the barrel. Then, I pulled a plug on the lower side to drain the dirty water. Fresh water for the rinse was added using a garden hose. More agitation with the paddle followed. Finally, I would feed the clothes through a ringer with one hand while turning the crank to squeeze them through with the other hand.

Today, I felt like I had been through that ringer. My muscles screamed at me to sit down, and my eyelids followed with a plea to close them.

*Soon. Be patient. I'm almost done with this day.*

An old car driven by a man I had never seen chugged into our yard. He had a head full of wavy gray hair, and the wrinkles on his face gave him a distinguished, handsome appearance. After sliding out of his car, he slammed the door. Then he approached me like a puppy who had eaten the plate of hamburgers on the counter. Before he said a word, I could read the expression in his eyes.

*Another unannounced overnight visitor!*

Once again, our home in Kumasi, Ghana, was the perfect stopping place for missionaries traveling between the capital, Accra, and Tamale in the north. Tamale was the center for several mission organizations, including the Ghana Institute of Linguistics (GIL), an arm of Wycliffe Bible Translators.

Hosting fellow missionaries was a pleasant interlude to our life in Kumasi: we enjoyed fellowship, games, and swapping life stories and prayer requests. This day, however, I was too exhausted to accommodate a surprise visitor. Selfishly, I thought about my need for rest and renewal rather than this stranger's needs.

Sam Moncrieff was today's visitor, a short-term builder in Africa, coming out on his own time and using his own savings to facilitate building projects in Tamale. Sporting the rugged face of one who works in the sun, his gentle smile seemed the opposite of his tough-man exterior.

Sam introduced himself, explained how he had been told about us, and asked if he could stay one night with us.

"Of course." I tried my best to say yes to whatever God brought to me, even when it was an unexpected interruption in my plans. But as I know all too well, "yes" with a cheery voice didn't necessarily mean "yes" with a good attitude.

My attitude improved quickly as I showed Sam the guest room and brought him towels. His gratefulness was contagious. "This is perfect," he said, glancing at the simple accommodation as if I had offered him an ocean-view room in a five-star hotel. I could tell he was a godly man who didn't want to be a bother.

I set another place at the supper table. During the meal, Sam interacted with our three kids (ages twelve, ten, and nine). I was touched by how caring he was to each of them. He stepped into a grandfatherly role, speaking truth into their young lives.

The following day, I served a breakfast of eggs and grits. Afterward, we stood around his car while Mark prayed for his trip and ministry. "Sam, plan to stay when you are headed back to Accra. We can be your Kumasi home." I hoped we would see him again. The footprints he left on my heart were ones of the joy he had in serving Jesus wherever he was—whether on top of a building with a hammer or in the home of a tired missionary.

I went to the guest room to collect the linens to wash, and there Sam had left a thank you note on the bed and some money "to help with the cost of food."

I was humbled. *What a kind servant of the Lord.*

About a year later, God moved us to Tamale. We got to know Sam better when he came from the U.S. for a few months of building projects during the summers.

Sharing a meal was always special. It wasn't one-sided with us having him over for a home-cooked dinner. Not at all. We were just as often the recipients of Sam's culinary skills.

One evening, when he hosted the five of us in his small apartment, he prepared homemade tomato soup and freshly baked bread. After eating, we watched *The Apple Dumpling Gang* on his portable VCR. It felt like a family night at Grandpa's house.

When asked why his wife Julie wasn't with him on each trip, he casually mentioned that she was taking care of some of their rental properties. This should have indicated that Sam was a man of significant means. It didn't cross my mind, though. And Sam was so unpretentious and humble that his bank account did not affect his character.

Sometimes Julie came with him, so it was fun to get to know her too. She treated us like long-lost friends, with the same heart as Sam.

Julie enjoyed crafts and sewing. She surprised our daughters with handmade Cabbage Patch dolls, wearing actual baby dresses and tiny patent-leather shoes. When we adopted two motherless girls from the orphanage in Tamale, Julie made Cabbage Patch dolls for them too. She made their dolls with the same hair and skin color God had given them.

We were blessed to have Sam and Julie, these two angels, in our lives during their summers in Tamale.

Our mission board required us to raise monthly support. God blessed us with a faithful support team, but with the cost of living increasing and loyal supporters leaving this earth to meet their Maker, adding to our support base was an ongoing process.

One day, I was reading over our monthly donor report, scanning the names as I thanked God for each one. I inhaled sharply when I saw Sam and Julie Moncrieff on the list for $100 support. That was the first of many years of monthly support from these angels.

In 1997, God led us to a new ministry with DiscipleMakers on college campuses in the northeastern part of the U.S. The Moncrieffs continued to support us in our new ministry.

The following year, we traveled from Pennsylvania with our two youngest daughters to visit supporters in California. We spent time with the Moncrieffs in their San Francisco home and at their Mount Hermon mountain cottage. To end our time together, we traveled in their RV to Anaheim to enjoy a few days at Disneyland. They treated us like their own children and grandchildren.

Fast-forward to 2008. My husband was serving as the missions pastor at a church in Wisconsin. His position was salaried, so we no longer needed monthly support. Our friendship with the Moncrieffs continued because we were true soul mates. We related to them in a more profound way than just a missionary/supporter relationship.

One morning in the fall of that year, one of our teenage daughters came into the kitchen rubbing her left eye. "Mom, my vision is still blurry," she complained. "Something is wrong." I assumed she needed to change her contacts, but the complaints continued.

After a week of this, I realized her eye condition could be serious. I called an ophthalmologist for the next available appointment. The doctor had a cancellation for that afternoon—another instance of God at work for us.

The doctor examined her and then spoke privately to me. Her eyes met mine, and in a quiet voice, the doctor said, "Your daughter has optic neuritis—a presenting symptom of multiple sclerosis. I want to order an MRI of her brain."

My heart plummeted to my feet. *MS is serious! How can one so young have MS? And what about the cost of an MRI?*

My trembling hand held the slip of paper with the neurologist's contact information while I called Mark. Our daughter was getting blood work done, and I wanted to talk to him before calling the next doctor, worried for our daughter.

I knew God would provide the funds for the MRI. *But how?*

I emailed our family and close friends about this faith-stretching trial, asking for prayer, wisdom, and God's healing touch.

I got a fast response from Sam and Julie.

"Amy, get the MRI. We will pay for it."

Emotional exhaustion permeated my body. A possible serious illness of one's child does that to a parent. As I sat in my office chair rereading Julie's email, I remembered a day of physical exhaustion twenty years earlier when Sam Moncrieff showed up at our home.

Indeed, I had entertained an angel unaware that day!

Hebrews 13:2: Do not neglect to show hospitality to strangers, for thereby some have entertained angels unawares.

# God's Protection in Travel

# Chapter Seven

# Travel Didn't Go As Planned

**June 1975 ~ Djibouti**

MIDWAY THROUGH OUR ONE-DAY trip to Djibouti to get my visa, a wrench was thrown into our plans. Actually, it was more like a hand grenade.

Mark and I were newlyweds. After we were married in Addis Ababa, Ethiopia, we spent our first two nights at the swanky Hilton Hotel. Then, we took the more affordable route of two weeks at the mission rest home in Bishoftu. We were assigned a one-room cabin only a bit larger than our double bed. A communal bathroom, dining hall meals with the other missionary vacationers, and a breathtaking view of a crater lake rounded out our honeymoon experiences.

After our honeymoon, I was required to get an Ethiopian resident visa in my new name, Mrs. Mark Hagerup. This transaction had to take place in a different country.

We planned to fly into hot Djibouti and walk to the embassy to get the visa stamped in my passport. After that, we would continue to the station to catch the train back to Ethiopia the same day. The train only traveled to Ethiopia every other day, so we arranged to fly to Djibouti on a day when the train could take us back that same evening.

As we deplaned, the hot air hit us like we were entering a sauna. We moved sluggishly through the heat to reach the embassy by noon, but when we got there, we found they had closed for the midday siesta—for four hours!

We found a café where we indulged in two expensive Sprites, sipping them slowly to kill time. After delaying there as long as we politely could, we ventured out again and took shelter underneath a bridge. We rested there like two motorcyclists caught in a rain storm. But no refreshing rain fell—only scorching sunrays pouring down on us. Despite the high temperature, we snuggled and dreamed of our future together.

Finally, we returned to reality, gathered our belongings and almost empty water bottles, and returned to the embassy.

Unfortunately, other desperate souls had beaten us there. We edged our way into the crowd at the massive iron gate. No one was allowed access to the compound, so Mark stretched out his long arm, waving my passport through the bars, hoping the official would take it for that needed visa stamp.

After granting visas to a few Africans, the embassy personnel announced they would be closing for the day. Mark immediately begged for mercy in Amharic while I prayed. The official turned toward Mark's voice, hesitated, and took my passport from him.

We had waited hours for that coveted stamp, but it took only a few minutes for them to process it. The passport was soon back in Mark's hand. We accepted it with profuse thanks and then sprinted toward the train station. I was like a chihuahua trying to keep up with a Great Dane since my husband is six foot five inches to my petite five foot three inches.

Since we had done our homework, we knew the train to Ethiopia was scheduled to leave at seven o'clock. It was almost six p.m. when a curfew in the city went into effect. Cautioned to be off the streets due to the local unrest after dark, we had to hurry.

And then it happened: With our destination only a half mile away, we were horrified to see the train leaving the station. It was departing early because of the city's curfew.

We had missed it.

My trembling hand covered my mouth. Tears blurred my vision as we watched the train disappear behind some buildings while the sad whistle pierced the air.

"What are we going to do now?" I worried as I glanced at the overhead clouds. A gentle rain fell as if God was crying with me.

Because of the curfew, we knew we didn't have time to find a hotel. Nearby was a Catholic school with a wide sidewalk lined with giant shade trees, making the evening seem darker than it already was. With brave faces that neither of us was feeling, we walked up the sidewalk to the intricately carved wooden door and knocked.

The priest who answered couldn't understand our English as we pleaded for a night's refuge. Since Djibouti is French speaking, finding someone who could speak English to interpret for us was difficult.

Finally, a beautiful Ethiopian woman named Marta passed by on the sidewalk, on her way home. Her almond-shaped eyes dominated her petite face, and her gold hoop earrings gave her a professional appearance. Marta must have been touched by our efforts to communicate in English because she climbed the steps beside us. She knew English and interpreted for us. Her earnest tone and wild hand gestures begged on our behalf as if she were our mother.

At first, the priest was annoyed and said (through Marta's interpretation), "I know kids like you—you say you want to stay for the night, and then you stay for a month!" We were only twenty-four and twenty-one, and no doubt reminded him of wayward young moochers he had tried to help in the past.

We had enough money to stay in a hotel, so cash was not the problem. Because of the curfew, we desperately needed a place to spend the night in safety.

The priest escorted us to the gate, shaking his head, refusing to accommodate us. But God softened his heart at the last minute.

Stopping abruptly as if he had run into an invisible wall, he seemed to have a change of heart and motioned for us to follow him. Back down the sidewalk we went and then ascended the steps of another building. Unlocking the door, he ushered us into a spacious hallway with doors on each side. He led us to a traditional classroom, turned on the light, and said something in French as he swept his arm to indicate the availability of this desk-filled room.

Marta had followed us inside, earning the title of guardian angel. When she saw the classroom as our offered refuge, she looked horrified. Her staccato French in a higher-than-normal pitch showed what she thought of this room as our sleeping venue. My new husband and I were satisfied—we would be safe from the rain, the bugs, and the police. We could curl up together on the floor and wait for daylight to find a hotel.

Marta thought otherwise. She turned to us and said, "This isn't good. Where will you wash? Where will you sleep? No, you can't stay here. Come with me. You can stay at my house."

We tried to refuse, saying we could manage with the room for one night, but she insisted we follow her.

Thankfully, the rain had stopped. Marta marched ahead of us with determined steps as the street became enveloped in darkness. We didn't know if we were going to a mud hut or a mansion; we trusted our guide and were humbly grateful.

Because we had emptied our water bottles earlier, my throat was parched. I knew we were being led to safety and, hopefully, clean water to drink.

Marta was married to George, an Italian who owned the Pepsi factory in Djibouti. She led us to her spacious house where she and George lived with their four teenagers. Mark and I collapsed on the sofa, content to be safely off the street, while they brought us Pepsi after Pepsi. We gratefully drank four or five each.

When they asked us about eating dinner, we insisted we weren't hungry—*how could we take advantage of their hospitality to give us lodging by accepting food, too?* But when they served supper, they invited us to join them at the two empty chairs they had added to the table.

Their kitchen worker served us spaghetti—the best I'd ever eaten. I was so hungry that I had two generous portions, not realizing that the spaghetti was the appetizer. After the spaghetti plates were cleared, we were served steak and baked potatoes.

George and Marta told us they would sleep in their kids' bedrooms and give us their room. This was a radical upset of my belief system. *The owner of Pepsi in Djibouti is giving his bedroom to total strangers off the street?* My eyes widened as I glanced at Mark. He had the same incredulous look on his face. *Can you believe this?* I tried to communicate with him through rising eyebrows. He acknowledged me with a twitching smile.

Djibouti is so hot at that time of year that water straight from the tap is scalding. Bathwater must be drawn in the morning to cool down enough to bathe by evening. Marta even gave me her cooled-down bathwater!

She pulled a delicate Somali nightgown from her closet and handed it to me. When I tried to put it on, my head was too large to fit through the neck opening. Marta had a solution: she took the gown from me and ripped it to make more room for my head. Meeting the needs of her guests was more important to her than preserving the value of a nightgown.

After everyone left for school and work the next day, we found a nearby shop and bought a French Bible. We returned to their home and left the Bible on the table with a note of thanks, telling them we were going to a hotel for our second night.

We hired a taxi to transport us back to town where we found a hotel. After surrendering our passports to the front desk clerk, we were directed to a modest but clean room on the second floor. I plopped my oversized purse on the bed and pushed the sheer curtains back to see the street below us. I felt a tender arm around my waist as Mark joined me to take in the view.

A loud pounding on our door jolted us from our serene moment. I flinched and clung to Mark. He was calm and gently removed my arms while he went to answer the knocking.

There was Marta, hands on her hips, with the sheepish hotel manager standing beside her. She had gone home for lunch, found our note, and come searching for us.

"You must come back to our home. It will be better for you," she told us sternly as if she were a mother hen scolding her wayward chicks. We might have felt like wayward chicks but we were loved and cherished ones.

Marta demanded the manager return our passports without charging us since we hadn't used anything. Then she paid a taxi to drive us to her house. We watched the scenery speed by as we were whisked back to God's provision of our temporary home in Djibouti.

We enjoyed another evening of abundant food, a steady supply of Pepsi, cooled-down bath water, a custom-torn nightgown, and an air-conditioned bedroom—all for us.

And so we spent our second night at George and Marta's home.

As I snuggled into the white pillowcase, I ran my fingers over the embroidered threads and thought, "Such finery!" A simple pillow would have been sufficient, but God supplied more than needed: He provided finery. This is God's abundant, lavish provision for us—His naive, baby missionaries in a strange country.

I could almost hear God say, "Look how I handled this trial. Notice how I provided for you. This is just the beginning. I have much more in store for you and Mark.

"Don't worry. Trust Me. And behold my wonder. Every. Single. Time."

1 Corinthians 2:9: But, as it is written, "What no eye has seen, nor ear heard, nor the heart of man imagined, what God has prepared for those who love him."

# Chapter Eight

# Lesson Learned from a Mule

**October 1976 ~ Waka, Ethiopia**

DURING OUR FIRST TERM in Ethiopia, Mark and I were assigned to the remote village of Waka, which was not accessible by a car road. When we moved there, we had been flown in by MAF. We landed on a short, grassy airstrip, one hike-able mountain from where we would live and work. To hike from the airstrip down the valley and up the next hill took about forty-five minutes. The compound consisted of two missionary homes, a missions elementary school, a Bible school, and a clinic. All around us were other Ethiopian homes, too.

Mark's responsibilities included teaching at the Bible school and trekking with church leaders to rural areas to teach God's Word. Some of these excursions would take two or three days to get to their destination, leaving me alone with our baby for five days or more.

Mark was preparing for an exceptionally long trek to Yeli—three days one way, which meant seven days away. I sat on the bed with my legs drawn up under my chin as I observed him roll up his sleeping bag. Feeling the need to be supportive, I wiped my tears and asked how I could help him prepare.

Stopping mid-roll, he moved toward where I was sitting. His eyes met mine, and I could see compassion in them. "Amy, why don't you and Benjy come with me?"

That was the craziest thing I had ever heard! *How can I take an eight-month-old baby on a seven-day trek riding mules and walking for miles through mountains?*

But my heart overruled my mind's tendency to preplan everything, and I blurted out, "Let's do it!" before practicality won over my brain.

Mark had never been to this area before. The trek involved hiking some of the time and riding hired mules the rest of the time. We rose early the following day to start our adventure.

We were surrounded by rocky mountains, with clouds sitting on their tops like whipped cream. At the base of the mountain, wildflowers and bright, green foliage were abundant. But as we ascended, the landscape became sparse, with howling winds nipping at our clothes. I marveled at the absence of litter or billboards as far as my eyes could see—just God's dazzling handiwork all around us.

When evening came, we stopped at a local church and set up our sleeping bags to spend the night. Women from the church prepared food over open fires for their unexpected visitors. African hospitality was so delightful. We were the privileged recipients of it many times.

Reaching our destination on the third day of our trek, we were greeted by the whole village. We met sisters and brothers in the Lord we didn't know we had. Curious children tiptoed to me to touch my white skin or feel Benjy's silky hair. After eating, we gathered for the real food: God's Word. I noticed how all work—cooking, sweeping, carrying buckets of water—halted to focus on God's truths taught in the Bible.

On the fifth day, the amber sun beckoned us to wake up and prepare for our trek home. Our Ethiopian brothers said they knew a shortcut we could take—getting us back to Waka in two days instead of three. That sounded great to us.

On the return journey, we laughed, told stories, and listened to nature's symphony. The mountains were never silent: the rustling of the trees was punctuated by bird calls and occasional scurryings of some unseen creature in the dry grass. After a fatiguing day, we arrived at another church to stay our final night on the road—or the trail, as the case was for us.

The morning sun greeted me as I gently awakened our baby in my sleeping bag. Hot porridge and coffee had been boiled for us. We sat in a circle, filling our bellies with sustenance before embarking on the final leg of our trip. Soon, we were on our way.

I clutched my eight-month-old as the mule clomped along the mountain path. Benjy was tied to me with a cloth baby carrier. The makeshift seat belt allowed me one free hand to hold onto the saddle's horn while my other hand held his little body to keep him from jostling.

I gazed over the hundreds of shades of green down the mountainside to my right—towering trees, tiny plants, and every size in between. While savoring the forest smells of damp moss and wildflowers, my eyes feasted on a banquet of nature.

My mule's hoofs plodding on the path mimicked the rhythm of a ticking clock. I glanced over my shoulder and beamed at my husband, who was on a mule right behind me.

The steadiness of the mule's sure steps could have lulled me into a trance if it weren't for the terrain we were now encountering. *This is getting more precarious.*

The path was becoming narrower—shrinking before my eyes. To my left, the mountain was close to me, going straight up. I could put my hand on it. My left knee was bumping against it with each forward movement of the mule.

To my right was a sheer slope plummeting down to the valley below. I felt like I was on a high dive, staring at the water that seemed a mile away. Only there was no water down there—just an abyss of trees and rocks.

The hair stood up on my arms, and I shuddered. *What if I need to dismount? What if we want to turn back?*

My shoulders tensed. I gripped Benjy tighter.

I leaned toward the left side against the solidness of the rock wall as if that stability would support me if my mule lost his footing. It was a false sense of security: if my mule stumbled, Benjy and I would be hurtling down the mountainside on our unprotected side.

And then I saw it.

The path ahead was washed out—probably by rain, a rock slide, or both.

My mule would have to jump about three feet to continue on the narrow path.

*There is no way my mule can jump that monstrous gap!*

"Mark, I'm scared!" I quavered. "I don't know what to do!"

I didn't know if Mark could see the gaping hole in the path since he was behind me, but he could sense the terror in my voice. Benjy was fine, though; he was too young to know that his life was in danger. When he heard my trembling voice, Benjy craned his neck to gaze up at me with wide eyes; his chubby cheeks framed his trusting smile.

Mark answered, "Just hold on, Amy. Trust the mule—he knows what to do."

So I held on, and we jumped—trusting Benjy, the confident mule, and untrusting me.

And we made it.

My mule continued his steady clomping as if we were on some six-foot-wide trail and hadn't just jumped a precipitous ditch.

I glanced over my shoulder in time to see Mark's mule perform the same stunt and settle into his clopping gait.

I had no option but to put my complete trust in that mule—for my life and safety. There was nothing I could do to help the mule out. Nothing. Nada. Zilch.

Sometimes, my stress gives me heart-pounding, gut-clenching feelings—like I had on that mule. But God has promised never to leave me, whatever I am going through. I don't need to fear the outcome. God is in control, and He is better than any sure-footed mule.

Did God use a mule to teach me to trust Him more?
Why, yes—yes, He did!

Psalm 46:1–2: God is our refuge and strength, A very present help in trouble. Therefore we will not fear, though the earth gives way, though the mountains be moved into the heart of the sea.

# Chapter Nine

# Injured in the Middle of Nowhere

## November 1976 ~ Soddo, Ethiopia

"It seems like we must make the two-day walk back into Waka. There is no other option," Mark said as the screen door slammed behind him. He had come from consulting with Merle, the station head. We had flown to Soddo for Thanksgiving, and the government had grounded the MAF planes while we were there. We waited a few more days before concluding MAF would not be flying again anytime soon.

"No worries. Benjy traveled well on the mule to Yeli last month. I think he will be fine. Won't you, sweetheart?" I turned to face our nine-month-old son, who was playing with pots and spoons on the floor. Benjy had no clue that his parents were planning another grueling two-day trek. He trusted his parents would care for his needs. And he didn't have a vote anyway.

"Let's get our food and water ready. Merle said he would drive us to the bridge tomorrow," Mark continued. Our Waka coworker, Cathy, had been notified of our plans through the mission two-way radio. She would tell Daweet to round up mules with their owners to meet us at the bridge. Cathy, a nurse, had much more experience as a missionary than we did. We were glad to be stationed with her.

Merle drove his Land Rover as close as he could to what was left of the vehicle bridge over the crystal-clear river. One by one, the wooden planks that made the bridge base on top of the iron bars had been stolen—possibly for firewood. A vehicle could no longer drive over it. Even walking over it was precarious—carefully placing one's foot firmly on a metal bar before daring to move the other foot.

We waved to Daweet, Gulu, Lucas, and the others waiting on the other side, each with a mule beside him. These guys were great friends, walking miles to help bring us home. We hugged Merle and his wife, June, and Mark took Benjy from her arms. We thanked them and began our calculated walk across the so-called bridge as the gurgling water below us seemed to whisper secrets to the rocks.

After we hiked for three hours, the sun started to trade places with the moon. We stopped to spend the night with a local church family, whom Daweet had told that we would be coming. The believers were friendly, and the ladies had prepared the delicious national dish, *injera bu wut*. (Injera is a flatbread made with fermented tef. It is served with different spicy beans, vegetables, and meat stews on top.) After eating, we lined up our sleeping bags on the mud floor of the church. Our night-time preparations resembled a Scout troop out earning a camping badge.

Mark shook my shoulders to wake me early the following day. Our sleeping son was snuggled close to me on my makeshift bed. We had the longer stretch of our journey ahead of us. From Soddo to Waka was about forty miles as the crow flies. But my husband would always add, "But we don't fly like crows." We were able to get transport to the broken-down bridge, which got us within twenty miles or so of our home in Waka.

My mule seemed edgy that morning as Mark boosted me into the saddle and handed me Benjy. I wrapped my cloth baby carrier around him and tied his mule "seat belt" at my back. We felt like old pros at this after the recent six-day trek to Yeli.

The trees nodded their approval as God's morning star grew brighter on the path. Daweet led the way, followed by Mark on his mule. Benjy and I were next in line with more Ethiopian brothers and their mules behind us, carrying our water, food, and supplies.

About an hour into our trek, the landscape descended sharply toward a dried-up creek bed. I leaned backward to compensate for the downward movement of my mule. Tightening my grip on my son, I shifted in my saddle as we headed toward the bottom of the hill.

A herd of skinny cows descended toward us from the other direction. Young boys urged the cattle with cut-off branches to guide them. The herders aimed the cows to one side, which meant they would pass me on my right side, where the forest met the path. The cows approaching us were mooing their displeasure at finding mules and humans on their familiar trail.

When the cows reached me, my mule got spooked and swung around to head back up the trail we had come down. The cinch on the aging saddle gave way, sending the saddle, my baby, and me around the mule's belly. I tensed up, wrapping Benjy as best as possible to protect him. I landed on the small of my back on a flat-top boulder with Benjy on top of me. Pain shot through my back—a pain worse than labor.

Worry bolted through my mind: *I think my back is broken!*

Benjy's cry pierced the cool morning air, alerting the travelers ahead of us to our plight. Mark dismounted, rushed to my side, and untied the cloth baby carrier. When he lifted our son from on top of me, Benjy stopped crying. That was a relief—he was scared, not physically hurt.

The story was different for me, though: I was in excruciating pain. It felt like all the vertebrae in my back were now in a zigzag pattern. The young men traveling with us gathered around me, crying, "Way-nee, way-nee, way-nee," an Ethiopian expression of distress.

Mark tried to help me to my feet, but I screamed in agony. Lucas grabbed a sleeping bag off one of the mules. He and Mark stuffed it around me to give me a cushion as I lay immovable on the massive rock. My husband led us in prayer, asking God to heal me and to give us wisdom on whether to proceed into Waka or to return to Soddo, where there was a mission hospital.

Lifting his head after saying "amen," Mark knelt beside me. "We'll try again in thirty minutes to see if you can stand. Try to rest, and don't worry."

But I did worry.

During that half hour, I gazed into the fair sky. My thoughts scurried like the little squirrels chasing each other across the path.

I worried that I might never walk again.

I worried that our missionary career could be ended.

I worried that I might not be able to have another child or care for the one we already had.

I worried about how long I would lie there.

I worried how a helicopter could land if needed to rescue me.

I don't remember trusting God to help me through this.

Oh, I remember praying for healing—that I craved.

*But what if He doesn't heal me? Will I still trust Him?*

The thirty minutes passed when I would try to stand up. Mark prayed again before the second attempt.

He reached for my hands as everyone watching held their collective breath.

Mark pulled me to a standing position while my back didn't complain. My feet were proudly bearing my weight as I balanced in an upright position. My face broke into a smile. *I can stand! Hallelujah! I am standing!*

I cautiously took one step. Then two. *I can walk! Praise God!*

Daweet, Lucas, and Gulu excitedly trilled their tongues to see me standing and taking tiny steps. I learned later that the trilling was an expression of excitement and happiness often heard at celebrations and weddings.

Daweet cut me a solid branch to use as a walking stick, and we decided to go to Waka rather than back to Soddo.

Once I found my walking rhythm on that mountain path, I thanked God. First, I thanked Him for my feet, legs, and back with properly lined-up vertebrae that worked. *How recently have I thanked Him for the gift of walking?*

Then I thanked Him for my eyes that I could see, my ears that I could hear, my mouth that I could talk and eat, and my voice that I could sing His praises.

I thanked Him for a nose to smell delicious bread baking, the scent of the hibiscus in our yard, and the aroma of juicy strawberries waiting to be picked.

I thanked Him for my hands so I could feel my baby's skin, write words of love to my mother in another country, and hug people He had placed in my life.

*Thank You, Abba Father. Life can change so quickly. I know I don't thank You enough. Thanks for giving me a "wake-up call"—or, more accurately, a "wake-up fall"—another chance to thank You. And I've only scratched the surface!*

We lumbered along through the mountains. All the men took turns carrying Benjy. My injury slowed our pace. I clicked along the path with my walking stick, making it sound like I had three feet instead of two. My cane helped me navigate the irregularities of the path, but it didn't help me go faster. In the middle of the day, I suffered from a heat stroke, so we rested for several hours. While we took our break, Gulu ran ahead to inform Cathy of my accident and ask her to send jackets, as the evening would turn chilly. After a few hours of sitting in the shade and indulging in some bananas brought to us by a mountain resident, we resumed our trek.

Gulu's swift feet carried the word to Cathy. As the sun turned in for the night, Gulu returned with jackets and a thermos of hot tea, warming our bodies physically and our hearts emotionally. We offered the tea to our fellow travelers, but they refused to take any for themselves.

We still had a few more hours to walk in the dark, but the lustrous moon cast an ethereal glow on the path. The mules didn't need assistance; they instinctively knew their way home—another wonder of God.

When we arrived at our four-room cottage, Cathy greeted us and helped us carry in our supplies. The radio was crackling with static, waiting for us to give the call sign to reach SIM in Soddo. Cathy had set up a radio standby with Dr. Bob Bowers. After questioning what happened and how I was doing, Dr. Bob instructed me to wrap my legs in ace bandages and keep them elevated. He set up additional radio standbys to talk again daily for a few days to be sure I was healing.

Amazingly, I had no recurring back pain. Once the soreness went away, I was fine. God had healed me. When I get to heaven, I will ask God if my back had been broken and He healed it.

But that doesn't matter. It also could have been God's plan to take away my ability to walk, and He still would be a good God. Perhaps He felt I wasn't mature enough in my faith to trust Him with a more "unfavorable-to-me" outcome.

There is so much in my life that I take for granted that subconsciously, I feel entitled.

On that mountain rock in a dried-up creek bed, God operated on my heart so I would acknowledge the privilege of every single breath He grants me.

After the operation, I stood up. I walked.

And I thanked God repeatedly for the privilege of life. *I still do.*

Psalm 150:6: Let everything that has breath praise the Lord! Praise the Lord!

# Chapter Ten

# Extreme Emotions at Airports

**September 1977 ~ Columbia, South Carolina**

As our plane descended to the Columbia airport, I felt like a five-year-old waiting for Christmas morning. My little son wiggled impatiently on my lap, which was reduced due to my pregnancy. Benjy tugged at his seat belt looped into mine. "No, sweetheart. You have to keep it on until the plane lands. Look at all those cars down there." I tried to distract him. How ironic that this same child who had been on multiday mule treks needed to be distracted to endure a plane ride.

Mark and I had married two and a half years earlier in Addis Ababa. None of our family members were able to attend our wedding. When Benjy was four months old, both my mother and Mark's brother had visited us in Soddo for a few weeks. Other than Mama and Scott, we had not seen any of our parents or siblings while we were in Ethiopia.

I had left my family in 1975 as a single girl and was returning—after completing a two-and-a-half year term in Africa—with a husband, a toddler, and baby number two on the way. So much in my life had changed, and so much in *their* lives had changed as well. Walking down the Jetway felt like going through a time tunnel where our lives would intersect again.

True to character, Mama threw her hands into the air and rushed toward me. I dropped the diaper bag and fell into her embrace. Rocky and Anna, my brother and sister, joined us, wrapping me in a cocoon of warmth. My sister Polly raced to Mark and reached out to take Benjy.

"Hi, Benjy," she whispered, trying not to overwhelm him. "I'm your aunt Polly, and this is your aunt Anna." Anna offered him the ribbons of colorful balloons she was holding. A smile blossomed on my face as I watched my nineteen-month-old son being showered with affection.

I thought of all the times I had dreamed of this moment of being reunited.

I was not disappointed!

Mark worked on his master's in missions degree at Columbia International University for that semester. We rented a mobile home near campus for those five months. Our second child, Deeanne, was born in December.

In early February 1978, we moved to the Chicago area near Mark's family and our home church. Our main supporting church in Arlington Heights gave us opportunities to report about our experiences in Ethiopia. We also explained that we were headed to Ghana in September with our same sending mission, SIM.

One bright Sunday morning, a couple approached us after the service. Gary Corwin, taller even than Mark, introduced himself to us. His wife, Dotsie, had long brown hair and sparkling eyes. "We were summer missionaries in Ghana with SIM," Gary said. "We plan to return to start a Bible college in Kumasi."

We were assigned to Kumasi, where they planned to work. "We will be coworkers then!" I said as I spontaneously hugged Dotsie. We listened to their experiences and imagined ourselves there in a few months.

They told us about Challenge Bookstore in Accra, a Christian store offering biblical literature to pastors and laypeople. Gary mentioned some of his Ghanaian friends by name. I could tell their hearts were still in Ghana. Dotsie continued, "There is an apartment above the bookstore where Dawn, a SIM missionary, lives. We became good friends with her, too."

From our years in Ethiopia, we knew missionary colleagues became close family. We looked forward to meeting Dawn and the other missionaries who were already there.

Preparation for our September departure included buying all we needed for our first four-year term. Mark worked for a local moving company—something he had done during college summers, which helped us pay for what we needed to purchase to set up house. Mark had to build wooden crates and gather fifty-gallon metal drums to pack everything. Then, they would be taken by semitruck to the port for travel by ocean freight liner to Ghana. We were blessed to have friends, including future colleagues Gary and Dotsie, helping us with all these preparations.

September 1978 ~ O'Hare Airport

In addition to emotional arrivals, airports are also places of solemn departures. Mark's parents sat in the connected, molded chairs, each with one of our children on their laps. I saw his mom wipe a tear from her eye. I could imagine how heartbroken I would have felt saying goodbye to my only two grandbabies, knowing I wouldn't see them again for four years. Also, I was five months pregnant with baby number three, so I'm sure they were thinking about that, too.

I took a deep breath and put my arm around Mark's waist. At least we were in this together. Knowing we were on our way to God's next assignment mitigated the pain of leaving loved ones.

We did the reverse steps of our arrival in Columbia twelve months earlier. Lingering hugs ended with boarding the Jetway to travel to a different world. Our families had embraced our return from Africa, and now they were letting us go again. Not only do missionaries give up a particular life, but their families who stay home also sacrifice closeness to their children and grandchildren.

We boarded the SIM charter flight to West Africa. This aircraft would be delivering missionaries to Liberia, Ghana, and Nigeria. As we settled into our seats, I looked around the plane at all my SIM family headed to their African lives. The camaraderie with fellow passengers was unusually high because everyone on board was a missionary. It didn't take long for deep sharing to occur all around us as people got to know each other.

The first destination was Liberia, where we said goodbye to new friends. The next stop was Ghana, our new home. Once we got through customs, our SIM missionaries in Accra would meet and take us to the guest house before our trip to Kumasi. I was exhilarated but apprehensive about new people, places, and culture.

As we neared Accra, the pilot came on the intercom. "I'm sorry to inform you that the Accra airport is temporarily closed. I am rerouting us to Abidjan. I will give you more information as it becomes available. Please stay seated with your seat belts fastened."

My worries popped up their ugly heads. *Where will we sleep? How will we get food for our children? How will our Accra SIM family find out where we are?*

Once we deplaned in the neighboring country of Ivory Coast, we were led to a counter where we were given hotel vouchers. That was a relief. Safely in the hotel room, we settled into the two beds—each of us with one child.

The following morning, our eight-month-old daughter needed milk. After she was born, I had breastfed her for six months. But with another pregnancy, my milk supply had dried up. We found a little café in the hotel, but Mark and I didn't speak French. We communicated that we wanted to order milk by pointing to the empty baby bottle. The server brought us a glass of milk on a silver platter. God fulfilled His promise to provide our daily bread—or milk, as the case may be.

Later that day as the golden sun dipped toward the horizon, we received word that the Accra airport had reopened. Our flight was scheduled to leave at eleven thirty p.m. We maneuvered our carry-ons and two babies onto the shuttle and then sped toward the airport. Stars pierced the black African sky, winking at us as we headed to the plane that would take us to our new life in Ghana.

Abidjan to Accra was going to be a short one-hour flight. I carried sleeping Deeanne, and Mark carried inquisitive Benjy as we boarded this final leg of our journey. My insides were a kaleidoscope of emotions: anxiety, curiosity, fear, eagerness, and concern. I took a few calming breaths and prayed for strength.

My fingers caressed our sleeping daughter's face. She didn't know where she was going but knew she was safe with her mommy. That was all the security she needed. On the other hand, I needed more knowledge to feel secure. The landing strip's flashing red lights through my porthole to the outside jolted me from my introspection. *We will soon be safe in our SIM host's guest room.*

One fifteen a.m. is an insane time to arrive at a destination. *Who wants to drive through the middle of the night to pick up the new missionaries?* But we were grateful to be safe at the end of our journey, even though the wee hours of the morning darkened our reception.

African airports were familiar to us since we had been missionaries in Ethiopia. But we had never been to Ghana. Once we finished going through customs with all our baggage, we bustled into the crowded taxi park. We scanned the arrivals area for other white faces, but there were none.

Without cell phones or easy access to flight information, our receiving missionaries had no idea when we would arrive. They were probably blissfully sleeping.

Every taxi driver near us wanted our business—some of them grabbing our bags to load into their vans before we had hired them. Trying to keep our bags safe added to our stress.

We didn't know where to tell a driver to go anyway. We had no address scribbled on a card in case the unthinkable happened, and no one had come to pick us up. We had no phone number to call. Nothing. My carefully laid contingency plans didn't exist. (I was still naive when it came to this type of thing, but I learned fast for future trips.)

A sinking feeling gripped me at the seriousness of our plight. This wasn't like our time in Djibouti when it was just me and Mark. We now had two babies in our care.

Tears pooled in my eyes as I absorbed the whole situation: middle of the night, luggage piled around us, two cranky babies, and one unflappable husband who was clearly flapped.

*What can we do?*

And then I remembered!

Our church friends Gary and Dotsie, who had been in Ghana, mentioned an apartment above the Challenge Bookstore where Dawn lived. We could go there.

Mark asked one of the taxi drivers, Kofi, if he knew of Challenge Bookstore. He did. Kofi got our business that night.

Our driver sped through the deserted streets of Accra. Sitting in the back seat, I felt all the swerves and potholes. Even though I was fighting to keep my eyes open, my new location zipping by my window had me riveted: colorful umbrellas over now-empty tables, shops with their front windows covered for the night, hardworking women with their wares on their heads going to their middle-of-the-night destinations.

Finally, Kofi stopped and turned off the engine. The Challenge Bookstore sign was visible at the front of the store. I craned my neck to examine the top floor: sure enough, an apartment appeared above it.

Stairs along the side of the store showed us that we didn't have to access the store itself to get to the apartment. Mark bounded up the stairs two at a time: his family's needs were a big part of his motivation. He pounded on the door while Benjy clung to his neck.

Now about three a.m., a sleepy Dawn cautiously cracked the door, then swung it open wide when she saw Mark. "I am so glad to see you. We have been praying for you to arrive safely. And now you are here," she said all in one breath while capturing our family in a group hug.

Dawn came down the stairs with us and gave Kofi the address of our mission leader's home, which was used as a guest house. The enthusiastic reception was repeated a few kilometers away at the Andersons' home. Warm embraces melted away the trauma of the last two hours. Joy-infused words from "up-until-now" perfect strangers tumbled into my ears: "You are here! Welcome to Ghana. We have been praying for you."

*Hello, SIM Ghana family!*

Thus, we began our first four-year term in Ghana (which turned into twenty years total). God always directs our paths—the major, the daily, and the unusual—like not knowing where to go in a strange country when one is not met at the airport.

Glimpsing in the rearview mirror, we saw how God directed us that scary night by some casual information shared five months earlier in the noisy church vestibule. *What a wonder God is!*

Proverbs 3:6: In all your ways, acknowledge him, and he will make straight your paths.

# Chapter Eleven

# How God Used a Vanity License Plate

**Summer 1991 ~ Champaign-Urbana, Illinois**

MARK'S DEJECTED FACE SHOWED the weight of his regret. "How could I have been so afraid?" he grumbled as he drove along the Illinois highway. He had worked at a grocery store during college and never shared his faith with his boss. Now, he was mourning what he felt was a forever-lost opportunity.

At our son's request, we were traveling to Champaign-Urbana to investigate the University of Illinois as a potential college for him. Ben and our girls had returned to Africa in time for the start of boarding school. Mark and I had two more months of furlough, so we visited supporters while checking out U of I (Mark's alma mater).

Mark perked up when he saw the Eisner grocery store where he had worked as a stock boy. "Who knows? Maybe my boss still works there. Let's stop and see." Richard Lehigh had been an excellent employer, but Mark as a new believer couldn't get up the courage to witness to him. Now, more than twenty years later, Mark still had a burden to share Christ with him.

We selected some fruit and got in the line to check out. Mark pulled out his credit card while querying the clerk if Richard Lehigh still worked there. She said, "Yes, he does, but unfortunately, he is not in today."

The girl waiting behind us heard Mark's question and said, "Richard Lehigh is my dad!" We were shocked that his daughter was in line behind us. Mark asked about Richard and told her to greet him from Mark Hagerup—even though her dad probably wouldn't remember him.

As we drove away, Mark continued to lament he had never shared his testimony with Mr. Lehigh—he had lost the opportunity, and now it was gone forever.

We headed to the College of Engineering at the university, where we had an appointment with a professor who was taking prospective students and other parents on a tour of the campus. While we were walking between buildings, the professor said to our group, "In the future, when we give group tours, every person will have a miniature computer in their hands." My husband told me he felt that was a bit unrealistic.

After the tour ended and we thanked our host, we headed out of town to our next destination—some supporters. We decided to stop for dinner after travelling on the highway about forty-five minutes. As we approached the traffic light on the exit ramp, we surveyed the restaurant choices. Big Boy's, one of our favorites, was the winner.

As we entered the restaurant, the smell of hamburgers and fries welcomed us. We were soon seated at the front window and ordered our food, with this cloud of regret still hanging over Mark.

From the booth where we were seated, I peered outside and noticed the license plate of a white car parked there. I said to Mark, "How do you spell Lehigh?" He spelled it out for me, and I said, "You mean like that license plate?"

He turned his attention to where I was pointing, and sure enough, there was an Illinois license plate with "LEHIGH" written in bold letters. Mark's eyes sparkled, and he grabbed my hand.

"I can't believe Mr. Lehigh could be here right now!" Mark said. After all, we were now about thirty miles away from Champaign-Urbana. Mark glanced around the restaurant but didn't spot his former employer. We kept our eyes trained on the car, waiting for the owners to come out to it. When they came out, Mark shouted, "That's him! Pay the bill, Amy—I can't miss this chance again."

Mark sprang from our booth and rushed outside. He caught Richard as he was closing his door. "Mr. Lehigh? Hey. Remember me? Mark Hagerup. You were my boss back in the seventies." His words burst out like machine gun fire.

"Yes, Mark. Of course, I remember you: the tallest, blondest worker I ever had."

After Mark briefly shared the gospel, Richard told him he had given his life to the Lord a few years earlier. His wife jokingly scolded Mark. "You should have told him back then, but he has found Jesus now."

What a comfort to Mark to know Richard was a brother in Christ. God had used another witness in his life to bring him to a saving knowledge of Him.

God, in all His sovereignty, had brought us to the same restaurant at the same time as Richard Lehigh. He orchestrated exactly where Richard would park. God had us seated at the perfect table so we would see Richard's license plate.

Many "God-incidents" had been divinely orchestrated to bring about His perfect will for us to meet up with Richard. God's plan for this meeting wasn't to see Richard come to know the Lord. Instead, it was for us to see how our faithful God had brought Mark's former boss to Himself through another witness.

We are responsible for sharing our faith, but we are not the ones who do the saving. God does that. When we fall short of sharing or don't see a favorable response, our primary responsibility is to continue to bring that one before the Lord in prayer.

God can raise another witness to share with the ones He knows will choose to be His children. Just like He did for Richard.

1 Corinthians 3:7: So neither he who plants nor he who waters is anything, but only God who gives the growth.

# Chapter Twelve

# Deadly Detour: Following the Wrong Leader

**May 2016 ~ Midwest Trip**

"Slow down!" I called out to my Yaris's empty passenger seat as I accelerated. I was trying to reach the moving truck ahead of me, traveling in tandem. "You are going too fast!" My words bounced around my empty car.

The blue and yellow Penske rental truck was about 500 yards ahead of me. The driver of that truck, my husband, must have mistakenly thought I was ahead of him instead of behind him. The blackbirds with their orange neckties were perched along the power lines as if giving an audience to my futile pursuit.

Mark was undoubtedly going as fast as he could to catch me.

*How can I catch him before I need more gas?*

Our daughter, Kinza, had just completed her master's in collaborative piano at Illinois State University. A self-starter, she had landed a job at a public high school in Indianapolis, and was now moving there.

When she was seven, we had bought a used upright piano so she could take lessons. God put a musical talent into Kinza, blossoming into piano playing and composing music. As a child, she loved practicing so much that sometimes I would forbid her to play the piano as a "time-out" for misbehavior. During her high school years, we told her that when she got an apartment of her own, we would give our piano to her.

Now we were making good on that promise. The piano and other furniture for her apartment were anchored inside that Penske truck ahead of me.

We were traveling to her apartment in Normal, Illinois, to load up the rest of her possessions and relocate her to Indianapolis. After unloading the Penske truck, we could return it in her new city and drive back to our home in Wisconsin in my car.

Mark had our GPS tracker in the truck, so I followed him. Our cell phones did not yet have navigation capabilities. Miles clicked by as we drove alongside vast cornfields. Giant white electric turbines rotated in the wind, reminding me of modern-day windmills. The Illinois landscape was calming to me.

All was going well until our two vehicles got separated going through the toll booth. I had our transponder with me so I could go through the fast lane. Mark, however, had to stop to pay the toll required for a truck. Once I realized that Mark had been delayed, I pulled over onto the shoulder to wait so I could resume following him.

Finally, I saw that blue and yellow Penske truck break free from the toll gate. That's when he took off at a fast pace. *I guess he didn't see me.* I wasn't worried. I watched the traffic to ease back onto the highway. I figured I would catch him soon enough.

I wasn't counting on him not seeing me, though. It seemed that he thought I was ahead of him and was going extra fast, trying to catch me. But I was behind him—by a long way!

Communicating with him was difficult. We both had cell phones, but operating them while driving—especially fast—took a lot of work. (There was no Siri or voice-to-text then.)

Finally, there were only five cars between us on a long stretch of highway where I could see far ahead. *Almost back together.* I blinked my lights, but that didn't help. He was still too far away and probably wasn't checking his rearview mirror.

I had reeled him into just one car between us, but I was far back. Beeping my horn didn't help except getting glares from drivers in passing cars.

I reached for my phone. *I have to do what I have to do. Help me, Lord.* I punched in his number, wondering if he could answer his phone. He had an old flip phone, so it took more work to answer a call than on an iPhone.

I could hear his phone ringing. Once. Twice. Then, "Hello?"

"Mark, I'm so glad you answered! I'm behind you!"

"You are?"

"Yes. I am not the car directly behind you but I am behind him. Can you see me?"

Despite this newfound knowledge, the driver of the Penske truck ahead didn't seem to be slowing down. He appeared to be going faster.

"Amy, you are not behind me. There is no Yaris behind me. I believe I am still behind you. I was at the toll booth a long time."

And then it hit me: I had been following the wrong truck!

When I pondered this travel blunder, I was reminded of when I was thirteen and our family was new to Columbia. Eager to make friends, I had latched onto a neighbor who was one year older than me: Susan.

Boys liked Susan. She owned all of the popular singing group Herman's Hermits' records, and her clothes were trendy. I wanted to be like her. Susan seemed to be a "good enough" girl. She didn't drink, smoke, or skip school. Her older brother was in a band, and her younger brother was my brother's good friend.

When I was fifteen, Susan invited me to attend a dance at the community center. I begged Mama to let me go, and she finally agreed. My insides vibrated like a plucked guitar string as I waited for Susan to pick me up.

At the dance, one of the band players kept catching my eye and winking at me. After the last song, he found me by the refreshment table and asked me to go out with him. I felt all tingly to be asked out by such a handsome guy. But when I opened my mouth to say yes, I heard myself say, "I'm sorry, but I can't." My mother was probably praying for God to protect me at that very moment. I was relieved that my mouth had said no.

Even though I belonged to Jesus, I wasn't following Him very well. I was following the wrong "truck" without even knowing it!

Mama taught me the importance of following the Lord with my life. She shared verses with me on being careful who I chose for friends. "I'm doing okay, Mama. Don't worry."

But then Susan offered me a copy of the health test from her previous year's class. "Here is your health test, Amy. Mr. Webb said that if a teacher is dumb enough to use the same test every year, it is perfectly fine to give it to someone who can benefit." I accepted the test from her. It wasn't cheating. Mr. Webb, another teacher, had said so.

But the following week, as I stared at my perfect test score, I couldn't shake off the suffocating blanket of moral failure.

Soon after that, when I was sixteen, a conference for high school juniors and seniors was held at Columbia Bible College near our home, and Mama wanted me to attend. Even though I didn't want to go, I wanted to make her happy because she always did so much for me. Reluctantly, I went.

That weekend, God spoke to me about refusing Him His rightful place on the throne of my life. I realized that I had Him in a closet. I would pull Him out only when I desired His help: to find another babysitting job or keep me safe while driving.

I invited God to be in the driver's seat of my life—I wanted Him to be my Leader. My life changed that weekend. I was eager to read my Bible and go to church. This feeling was different from being told what to do. It bubbled up out of me: to please God in everything.

I was eager to talk about my faith with my friends. I remember sharing the gospel with my close friend, Sheri, but I don't know if I explained it to Susan. We had grown apart over the recent months. I hope I told her. I am glad I can still impact her life by praying for God to bring another witness to her like He did for Mark's old boss.

When the conference ended, I sat on the sidewalk in front of the college administration building, watching for my mother's car. I thought about how I had been following the world's ways and had wandered from my faith.

God rescued me when I didn't even know I needed rescuing.

I was sincere in my followership, but I was sincerely wrong.

Just like what happened when I was sincerely following the wrong truck.

⟫⟫⟫  ⟪⟪⟪

I slowed down and scrutinized my rearview mirror for another Penske truck—one my husband was driving.

Sure enough—there he was behind me, starting to catch up.

Soon, we were driving side by side. I chuckled and waved as he passed me, taking back his place as my leader.

We arrived safely at Kinza's apartment—a blue and yellow Penske truck as the engine with a compact black Yaris as the caboose. I lingered in the car a few minutes, contemplating what could have happened. That wrong truck could have exited the highway with me in full pursuit. I could have gone a long way, even ending up at the wrong destination without knowing my error.

But God knew.

My heavenly Father saved me from that innocent mistake of following the wrong truck—just like He saved me from following the wrong person in my teens.

God is the perfect leader and has provided me with the best navigation tool in His Word.

Oh, and another great "correct Penske truck" is a godly parent.

John 8:12: Again, Jesus spoke to them, saying, "I am the light of the world. Whoever follows me will not walk in darkness, but will have the light of life."

# Section III

# God's Providence in my Childhood

# Chapter Thirteen

# The Impact of the Family Boss

**Summer 1959 ~ Atlanta, Georgia**

I WAS SIX WHEN I realized Daddy could make Mama cry.

It happened one Sunday afternoon when we all went to Papa's, my grandfather's, house. My dad had only one sibling, nine-year-old Stefan, who felt more like our cousin than our uncle. He had stayed with us for a few years after their mother died and before Papa remarried. Now, he lived with his dad and stepmom on the other side of Atlanta from where we lived.

Stefan had a miniature red car the size of a wagon that ran on a track on the hill behind their house. We took turns speeding down the slope and pushing that metal car back for another heart-racing, hair-blowing ride. After our outdoor play, we would head inside for snacks before piling into our real car to attend evening church.

But this Sunday, we were captivated by Papa's television set, a new addition to some middle-class homes. Even the commercials were fun to watch. They made me want to drink an ice-cold Coca-Cola. Our eyes widened when we saw the MGM lion roar, introducing

*The Wizard of Oz* coming on next. We had heard about this movie but had not seen it.

I heard Mama tell Daddy it would soon be time to leave for church. He turned his attention from her to us kids, then back at her again and said, "They can watch TV tonight. We can miss church." The three of us kids jumped up and down at his pronouncement. As I settled on the braided rug with the others, I searched the den for Mama but didn't see her. I wondered where she had gone.

I got up to find her, but she wasn't in the living room or the kitchen. My neck muscles tensed as I panicked. Perhaps she was on the screened-in porch, but the metal chairs out there were vacant.

Feeling my desperation rising, I twisted the basement door knob and opened the door just enough so I could peep into the dark, scary stairwell.

There she was—sitting on the steps, crying.

"Mama, what's wrong?" I choked out as I also started to sob. Whenever I saw her cry, I would dissolve into tears. I wanted to do everything I could to make her cheerful again. Her crying sucked the security out of me like a vacuum cleaner gobbling up spilled Cheerios.

Mama said, "Oh, sweetheart. Don't worry. I just wanted to go to church tonight."

As much as I desired to see *The Wizard of Oz* and was glad Daddy would let us watch it, I craved even more for Mama to be happy. Then, as she wiped her tears, she added, "But we will do what Daddy says."

Daddy was the boss, and with him as boss, going to church was optional.

November 1963 (age 10) ~ Tucker, GA

I believed that Daddy didn't like me.

When I sat behind him in the car and he wanted me to massage his neck, I didn't do it firm enough. I was the clumsy one when I spilled my milk. When my report cards were left on the table, only Mama read and signed them.

One chilly Saturday, I was surprised that Daddy was going to take us kids out for supper. Eating out was a rare treat. But Mama wasn't going to come with us for some reason. I wished I could stay home with her. There was no doubt in my ten-year-old mind that Mama liked me.

We followed my dad down the restaurant's steps to a massive black door with a fancy gold handle. I stared at the carved lion's head with its open mouth on the handle's top. I could almost hear it roar as the door squeaked on its heavy hinges. Once inside, it took me a minute to adjust to the darkness. I saw a long bar with many stools, but we were led to a regular table.

A person dressed up like a rabbit with long ears approached our table. Three-year-old Polly was shaking with fear. Anna held her protectively. She always did a great job hovering over Polly like a second mother. The bunny tried to be friendly, but none of us kids were impressed.

I surveyed the dark room, mostly filled with men drinking from heavy glass mugs with handles. An unfamiliar woman with thick red hair joined us at the table. Her name was Peggy, and she spoke to us in a high voice—as if we were babies. I wondered why she had come and sat with our family. I didn't want her there.

Polly started crying, so Anna gently rocked her and covered her eyes to shield her from the miserable place. When the food was brought to the table, Anna bribed Polly with a french fry to convince her to turn off her tears.

I also felt like bawling, but the fries comforted me, too.

I had been shaken up at school that week by President Kennedy's assassination. My fifth-grade teacher had pulled one of the big TVs into our classroom. We witnessed people huddled with their arms around each other on the side of the street. Police officers were jogging with their guns drawn. A bullet of dread had shot through my brain and I grabbed the girl sitting beside me. We held onto each other as we stared at the screen with our mouths hanging open.

The pictures told the story: One minute, our president was waving, and the next, he was slumped over in his convertible. It had happened so fast.

I was afraid something terrible like this might happen to Mama. When I got home from school that day, I rushed to her side. She reminded me of our faith in Jesus. I still felt safer in her presence, so I asked if I could stay home from school to be with her. She said no and read me some Bible verses about God being with me all the time.

All these thoughts flooded back as we sat in this gloomy, dim restaurant. Somehow, the darkness reminded me of death. I wanted to get back home to Mama. If I had been given a choice, I would have chosen to stay with her.

But I wasn't given the choice whether to go to that bar with Daddy and his girlfriend.

Because Daddy was the boss.

January 1964

I loved Saturdays—sleeping in was fun since there was no school bus to catch. Everything slowed down at our house. I took a deep breath and threw my covers off.

Daddy had arrived home late the night before. I'd heard him come in the back door, walk down the hallway, and open the door to his and Mama's bedroom. Mama must have been pleased that he came home because many nights he would never show up. I didn't know where he was staying. Mama seemed sad and always whispered on the phone to her church friends.

Daddy never paid much attention to me. He always told me to bring him his shoes or newspaper while Anna got to talk on the phone. I thought Anna was his favorite child. And my brother,

Rocky, once got to ride in the back of a pickup truck to my dad's sign shop. Daddy told me I couldn't go. Polly was a mama's girl, clinging to Mama whenever we were in public. Daddy ignored Polly.

I walked into our tiny kitchen with bare feet complaining about the cold linoleum floor. I was ready to say good morning to Daddy and Mama. But no one was there.

Daddy's chair was empty. He was always the first in the kitchen on a Saturday morning, with a cup of coffee in hand, sitting at the red Formica-topped table and reading the newspaper.

Then I saw them: four presents propped up against each other on the table. A folded piece of paper stood in front like a card for a birthday celebration. Except it wasn't anyone's birthday.

Anna and Rocky soon joined me from their bedrooms and stared at the presents. Polly was the last to come in, rubbing her sleepy eyes. When she saw the gifts, she said, "Oh lookie!"

Twelve-year-old Anna, the wisest of us all, seemed to understand the meaning behind Saturday morning gifts before my ten-year-old reasoning caught up. She spread her arms to shield the gifts, like an eagle protecting her young, and said, "Don't touch them. Mama might not want us to have them."

Mama soon came shuffling into the kitchen wearing terry cloth pink slippers. She lifted the folded paper and opened it. The brief note (I found out later) said something about Daddy leaving us, but she didn't read it to us.

We watched Mama for some clue as to what we should do. She gave a half smile but still didn't say anything. Reflecting on that, I think Mama wasn't surprised by Daddy's message. After a few minutes, Anna asked if we could have the presents. Mama came out of her silent pondering and said, "Of course you can have them!"

I picked up my gift—a Junior Scrabble game. It felt stiff as I ran my fingers over the words on the top. I liked word games; it was thoughtful of Daddy to get this for me.

I watched the others open their unbirthday gifts. Anna tore the box flaps that held a Beatles doll—she was really into the Beatles. Polly hugged her stuffed doggy, sucking on her thumb with her index finger hooked over her nose. If presents were supposed to be for celebrating, why did I feel so sad?

The oatmeal on the stove made that popping sound that happens when it is ready. Mama filled the bowls, setting one in front of each of us.

There was no room for a bowl at her spot. She had her Bible spread open on her placemat. Mama scooted her chair in and said: "Let's thank the Lord for our food, and then we will have our morning devotions." If Daddy had been present, we would have skipped Bible reading at breakfast. He didn't like that. We only did it when he was gone.

Thinking back on that fateful morning, I didn't feel devastated. I felt secure in Mama's love. As Mama started reading from Ephesians, I wondered if the presents meant that Daddy was officially gone this time—not just for a few days or a week.

And who would be the boss now?

March 1964

Those months after my father left were rough for my mother. After evening church one Sunday, we opened our car doors and saw bags of groceries piled on the back seat. Our squeals of delight could be heard at the other end of the parking lot. We helped Mama move them to the trunk as we peeked inside the bags. I was snooping for peanut butter. Sure enough—I spotted a gigantic jar. "Rocky, there is peanut butter!" I knew he would be excited too. He loved to put peanut butter and syrup on his pancakes, which I thought was a bit extravagant. I'm sure I had quirks myself, but I remember his better.

When we got home, Mama put away the groceries, thanking God as she stocked the cupboards. I asked, "Mama, are we poor?"

"Oh no, sweetheart. We are not poor. We are rich because we have Jesus."

I didn't feel rich, though.

Mama enrolled us in the free lunch program at our school. I felt embarrassed to have the lunch lady wave me through when the other kids had to present their punch cards. On hamburger days, I wanted to buy a second hamburger, but that was fifteen cents more. An extra hamburger wasn't available for those rich in Jesus but poor in lunch money.

After my dad left us, Mama filed to receive child support from him. She had to go to court to present her case. I wasn't there. I didn't even know she was going.

Years later, Mama told me about the hearing. She gave the judge all the details, including almost being evicted from our home and the heat being cut off. During her testimony, she saw the judge wipe tears as he turned his face away. He ordered my dad (who wasn't there) to pay monthly alimony.

But my dad did not obey.

No judge could boss him around.

September 1964 (age 11)

Anna turned thirteen and was driving me crazy. "I'm too sick to go to school," she said, pulling the blanket over her head as she turned over. But Mama made her go.

"Please, Mama, let me go to the party. All my friends are going," Anna begged. When Mama said no, Anna said, "You are so mean. You never let me do anything. I know Daddy would let me go."

But the most significant battle was on Sundays. "I won't go to church, and you can't make me!" Anna said for the second time that morning. Mama remained composed as she pulled out our maroon plaid dresses and placed them on my quilted bedspread.

"You don't have a choice, sweetheart. We are going to church as a family. We honor God when we worship Him with others. I love Jesus so much, and I pray that you will come to love Him too. Now get dressed and come to breakfast."

As Mama left the room, Anna made a sassy face, but she got dressed and went to church with us.

My favorite part of the week was being in church with Mama. Anna and I were on one side of her, Polly and Rocky on the other. I relished holding the hymnal and singing the hymns. During the sermon, I snuggled close to Mama, who was my whole world. I couldn't understand much of what the pastor said, but one thing was clear: Jesus loved me. He loved my mama, Anna, Rocky, Polly, and my dad, too.

Mama was the boss now, and attending church was no longer optional.

And that was because God was the Boss of Mama.

Psalm 107:41: He raises up the needy out of affliction and makes their families like flocks.

# Chapter Fourteen

# Mama's Desperate Christmas Eve

**Fall 1962 (age 9) ~ Tucker, GA**

FROM MY VIEW ON the front pew, where my feet could not yet reach the floor, I heard the harmony of my parents' voices. My dad was the minister of music, and my mom was the church pianist. Music was part of their makeup; they went together like peanut butter and jelly.

I listened to the familiar words while humming along quietly:

I'd rather have Jesus than silver or gold;
I'd rather be His than have riches untold;
I'd rather have Jesus than houses or lands;
I'd rather be led by His nail-pierced hands.

I saw my dad's arm around my mother's slim waist during their duet. When they finished, they smiled at each other before Mama returned to the piano.

I leaned back against the oak pew. To those watching, it appeared my parents loved each other and would rather have Jesus than anything else.

This was true for my mom. But it wasn't true at all for my dad.

Things were different at home, where his minister of music role was left at church, and there was no harmony with Mama.

At home, gentle words were met with hostile glares and silences. When I asked a question, I was told to leave him alone.

"Daddy will be home soon," Mama would say when she tucked us into our beds. But when I would get up for a glass of water, I'd see her kneeling in front of the sofa. The following day, his side of their bed would still be empty. This happened several nights each week.

On Christmas Eve that year, Mama kept peeking out the curtains to see if Daddy's blue Oldsmobile had pulled into the driveway. Finally, the headlights shone on the yard where the pavement ended, and my three siblings and I squealed that Daddy was home. We knew he was the one who bought the gifts for us.

We hung our stockings at our assigned spots and were herded to bed. After we prayed, Mama kissed us good night. Her eyes seemed glassy to me. *Were those tears?* She must have been so excited about our joy on Christmas morning that she couldn't contain her emotions. That must have been the reason for her tears.

But I wasn't sure.

Years later, I discovered that my father had arrived home that Christmas Eve without any presents. Mama shared their conversation from that heart-wrenching night with me.

When Mama realized my father was not bringing presents in from the car, she whispered: "Where are the children's presents, George?"

My dad said, "You have money from your piano lessons now. You can buy them presents. I never told you I would get the presents this year."

"But you always do. I assumed this year would be the same." Mama choked back tears.

"You assumed wrong," he said, stomping to their bedroom and slamming the door behind him.

With trembling fingers, my mother dialed one of her church friends. She had a few close friends who knew what was happening in her marriage. LaVelle and JoAnn (among others) were committed to praying and helping as they could.

When JoAnn answered, Mama could hardly get the words out between her desperate crying. "George didn't buy the children any presents. Please, can you help me?"

Her friends collected some items from their home, including a ukelele for me that LaVelle had restrung. JoAnn drove to our house, picked up my mother, and went to a twenty-four-hour drug store open on Christmas Eve. JoAnn probably paid for the items, too.

Christmas morning dawned, and four pairs of small bare feet gathered at the closed living room door. Our enthusiasm filled the air as we fought for the best position in the lineup. Anna, eleven years old, instructed us that three-year-old Polly would go first because she was the youngest. Anna told us she would go next because she was the oldest. I would follow third, and Rocky would be last. I was nine, and Rocky would turn eight in January.

When the door was opened, four starry-eyed children ran to their assigned stations on the sofa and chairs. I grabbed my stuffed stocking perched on the top of a few other presents on my chair. Candy and oranges tumbled out as I shook my embroidered ruby sock. Then, the ukulele caught my eye. I gingerly picked it up, and my fingers caressed the glossy strings—a real ukulele for me! My girlfriend, Charlotte, had one. Her dad, who we called Daddy Dean, had put new strings on it. Repairing musical instruments was his hobby. I couldn't wait to tell Charlotte I also had a ukulele.

Looking around the room at the bounty, I hugged my ukulele. I watched my siblings exclaiming over their new treasures. This was such a special day: everyone was happy.

I first headed to Daddy and squeezed his neck as I blurted out my thanks. He smiled a little but didn't hug me back. Then I rushed to Mama standing in the doorway. My exuberance almost knocked her down. "Thank you so much for everything, Mama!"

"God is so good," she murmured, crouching to hug me back.

*What a funny thing to say on Christmas morning*, I thought. But then Mama was always either talking about God or talking to Him. She was like that.

I took her face in my small hands and saw her eyes were glassy again like the night before. Only this time, I could see tears running down her cheeks. I reached my thumbs out on both sides of her face, wiped her tears away, and said, "Yes, Mama, God is so good to give me a mama like you."

I can now add, "And God is so good to give us precious friends like LaVelle and JoAnn to be the hands and feet of Jesus on a desperate Christmas Eve."

Isaiah 43:2, 5: When you pass through the waters, I will be with you, and through the rivers, they shall not overwhelm you . . . Fear not, for I am with you.

# Chapter Fifteen

# Doctor's Prediction I'd Go Insane

**May 1964 (age 10) ~ Tucker, GA**

GOING TO BED FELT like a punishment; I dreaded that time every night.

While my older sister, Anna, fell asleep quickly, I moved from one position to another, trying to get comfortable. I would be awake all night—at least, it seemed that way. The morning sun peeking through my sheer ivory curtains was the signal that I could finally get up.

One night, I noticed Mama tiptoe into our room, trying not to wake her two oldest daughters. She knelt at the end of my bed and rested her head on her crossed arms. I knew she was praying, but I didn't understand why she was talking to God in the middle of the night. *And why didn't she kneel at my sister's bed, too?*

After what seemed like half the night, she would get up and leave. Mama suspected I was sick.

As Mama prepared the eggs and toast the following day, I asked her why she had been kneeling at my bed. Her head jerked around from watching the frying pan. "You mean you were awake?"

"Of course. I'm awake every night."

"Oh, sweetheart, I must take you to the doctor." Mama, who grew up in South Carolina, always called us "sweetheart."

As I sipped milk from the Tupperware tumbler, my hand jerked, splashing some milk. I swiped at the spill with my napkin, pleading: "Mama, I feel fine. I don't need to go to the doctor. Really." But she insisted. I knew she cared for me.

Before giving in, I tried one more time: "Please wait until I get home from school." I hated to miss school, and the perfect attendance award was one way I could feel valued.

"I can stay home with her," my sister announced. Anna relished any possible reason for missing school. "I'll play Junior Scrabble with you, Amy, as long as you don't keep knocking the letters around like you did last time." I rolled my eyes at her, remembering our last game when I'd accidentally bumped the board, messing up the formed words.

Mama's wisdom and determination won out, like always. I never made it to school that day or for the remaining few weeks of school!

The doctor's stethoscope was draped around his neck, and he smelled like soap. "Hi. I'm Dr. Hawk. What's your name?"

"Amy." I clasped my hands tighter to stop their shaking. Doctors made me nervous; actually all men made me nervous—probably because of my absent father. Dr. Hawk asked my mother some questions, scribbling notes on his pad as if he would be tested on this information. This went on for ten minutes. I thought he had forgotten I was in the room too.

Turning his attention back to me, he listened to my heart. Then he watched my eyes, staring into them as if trying to see inside my brain. His face came closer to mine, which caused me to glance down at my hands. I smoothed out my wrinkled patient gown, trying to avoid his gaze. He said, "Amy, I want you to look at my nose." *That was easier since his nose didn't stare back at me.*

Next, he instructed me to grab his index and middle finger and squeeze as hard as possible. I obliged, but then he said, "Can't you squeeze harder than that?"

"I'm afraid I will hurt you if I do it harder."

Chuckling under his breath, he assured me I would not hurt him. I crunched with all my might, gritting my teeth for emphasis—*poor guy*. Mama told me later that I was hardly putting any pressure on the doctor's fingers when I thought I was "crushing the life out of them."

When the doctor had me place my hands on his open hands, they made little jerks even though I was trying to hold them still.

"Mrs. Roth," Dr. Hawk said, "I believe your daughter has St. Vitus dance, a disease of the nerves. Unfortunately, this disease leads to rheumatic fever, which can affect the heart. There are effective treatments, which I will start as soon as we confirm the diagnosis. I want to admit her to Eggleston Children's Hospital."

It's possible that I contracted the disease when I got scarlet fever and strep throat simultaneously. This could have resulted from me selling Girl Scout cookies in the pouring rain. My troop had been having a contest, and I wanted to win free cookies as the prize, showing my competitive spirit—and desire for sweets, too.

I later learned that St. Vitus dance, also called Sydenham chorea, is related to Huntington's disease, a rare disease that causes the breakdown of the nerves in the brain and can cause psychotic disorders.

The doctor motioned for my mother to step out into the hallway. I waited on the white-papered exam table, studying the cartoon figures on the wallpaper. I wanted to get to school. *What was taking so long?*

When my mother told me this story in my adulthood, she said the doctor told her I would probably go insane before I turned forty.

"Do you know how I responded?" she asked me with a twinkle in her eye. "I said to him, 'Oh, no, she won't.'" Her faith in God was strong, and she planned to plead with God for her daughter's stable mental health.

At the end of that day, I was lying in a hospital bed. The crisp white bed sheets crinkled beneath me as I rolled over in my prison. The guard rails felt cold when I touched them. *This is not fun.* My newly diagnosed disease caused insomnia. Another symptom was jerking hand movements and the inability to focus the eyes without darting from object to object. I fit these descriptions.

The ten-day hospital stay was amazingly pain-free until the very last day. I found out I would require concentrated penicillin shots every month until I turned twenty-two. These injections would protect me from getting rheumatic fever. My first 4 mL dose was on the last day of my hospital stay. At least I didn't have to take shots daily like my older sister, who had been diagnosed with type one diabetes a few months earlier.

Monthly shots felt like a death sentence, and eleven years until I reached age twenty-two seemed like an eternity. I also found out that I was to be confined to bed for three months. Our family planned to stay with my grandparents in South Carolina for the summer so Mama could renew her teaching certificate to get a full-time job. I would be trapped in my bunk instead of skipping down to the water fountain at the end of their street, which we loved to do. Gloominess pulsed through my veins with every beat of my heart.

When I got home from the hospital, I crawled into bed and snuggled into the bedsheets that smelled like lavender. No more nurse to wake me up to take my temperature. I wouldn't hear that boy across the hall crying—*poor little guy.*

I thought about what had happened this year: My dad left us in January. Anna was diagnosed with type one diabetes in March. And now I had been diagnosed with St. Vitus dance in May. Mama had been right: I was sick. I'm glad I could trust her to take care of me.

I groped for the Trixie Belden book I was reading. As I opened the bookmarked page, I heard Mama singing in the kitchen: "'Tis so sweet to trust in Jesus, just to take Him at His Word . . ."

I trusted Mama, and she trusted Jesus. At this time in my life, Mama was like Jesus to me.

Summer was over, and we were back in Georgia. I was no longer restricted to bedrest; the freedom to run around felt wonderful. I was ecstatic to be watching for the school bus again. Life had returned to some normalcy.

My blissful school days, however, were overshadowed by the once-a-month clinic visits. On a crisp autumn day, my mother drove me to my dreaded monthly shot. I rubbed my hand on the cotton, long-sleeve shirt on my arms—a sensation I savored. But that comforting touch didn't change my prickly heart. My forehead rested against the car window as we whizzed by the trees dressed in auburn and golden leaves. My eyes filled with tears as misery flooded over me.

I worked up the nerve to share my torment with Mama. "There are two things that make my life miserable."

"What are those things, sweetheart?" she said.

"My monthly shots and my piano lessons."

I was taking piano lessons and hated the daily practice. My mother was an accomplished pianist herself and taught lessons for some income. After teaching me herself, she had hired a friend to give me lessons, and I was not enjoying them at all—or at least the practicing part. Mama decided that day to relieve my anguish. She knew she couldn't stop the injections but she could discontinue my piano lessons.

As a side note, neither my accomplished piano-playing mother nor the piano-practicing complainer had any inkling that God would give me a daughter who became not only a piano teacher but also a lover of practicing.

July 1968 (age 15) ~ Columbia, SC

The summer before I entered seventh grade, we moved from Georgia to South Carolina, where my grandparents lived. Because Mama struggled to make ends meet, it made sense to be near her parents so they could help us.

Having moved from Georgia meant I transferred to a different doctor in South Carolina. By now, the shots had increased to two monstrous shots of 4 mLs each. The dogwoods were in bloom as Mama drove me to my new doctor. I had learned from Dr. Hawk in Georgia that taking penicillin daily in pill form was an option, but it was not available to me because, as a child, I might forget to take one.

At fifteen years old, I acted responsibly, with many babysitting jobs resulting from my own efforts. As a high school sophomore, I kept up with my grades, participated in a service organization called Anchor Club, and worked as one of the yearbook editors.

My mission that day was to convince Dr. Branham that I would be faithful to take that daily pill. Sitting in his office before the nurse prepared my injection, I passionately presented my case to him like a lawyer pleading her client's innocence. My mother, seated beside the examining table, nodded in agreement.

Dr. Branham believed I could be responsible for remembering my morning penicillin pill, so he prescribed multiple refills. I clutched that prescription like a million-dollar check written out to me.

On the drive home, the dogwood trees waved white flowers to our passing car. "Thank You, Jesus," Mama said as she turned a corner. I echoed her, "Yes, thank You, Lord."

I was one radiant teenager: no more monthly shots.

September 1970 (age 17)

With my senior year of high school looming, I began investigating a college path. *How can I afford to go to college?* We were poorer than field mice in the winter. My father never sent any support. My grades were As and Bs but not good enough for academic grants. Attending college seemed to be an impossible dream.

My mother learned about vocational rehabilitation, which offers scholarships to those with physical challenges. "Amy, listen to this," Mama said. She read aloud from the brochure: "We offer scholarships to the disabled, anyone with physical or mental impairment or on any daily medication required by a physician."

"Amy," her voice showed her excitement, "you are on daily medication required by a physician. You qualify to apply for this scholarship!" A tentative smile blossomed across my face as the reality of this possible funding took root. *This was incredible news!*

After applying for the VR scholarship aid, I received a call to schedule the complete testing. When the day arrived for the exam, I was as nervous as a cat meeting a cucumber for the first time. I sat at the cream-colored table, waiting for my tester to join me. The questions were straightforward, mostly being an oral test. There was a written portion that I don't remember well. Finally, it was over.

Then came the waiting part; the results would come in the mail.

After many disappointing trips to the mailbox, I saw the coveted letter between the bills and ads. My hand shook as I held the envelope with vocational rehabilitation as the return address, and I ripped it open. "We are pleased to inform you that you have been awarded a full scholarship to any school you choose for four academic years."

I hugged the letter, raised my gaze to the sky, and poured out my thanks to God.

I was going to college!

I graduated from Columbia Bible College in March 1975 with no school debt. In July of that year, I turned twenty-two, when I could discontinue the daily penicillin. I was on the medication just long enough to secure four years of scholarships. Once the pills stopped, I no longer qualified.

Despite the childhood disease of my nerves and the threat to weaken my heart, I healed well and am very healthy.

God brought good out of the illness He allowed in my life by using it to fund my college education. He had a plan all along. I have since learned to trust Him sooner—before I see His ultimate plan.

Oh, and I never did go insane.

Philippians 4:19: And my God will supply every need of yours according to his riches in glory in Christ Jesus.

# Chapter Sixteen

# When the FBI Came to Our Home

**June 1965 (age 11) ~ Tucker, GA**

About a year before my dad deserted our family, Mama found herself regularly begging him for grocery money. She had put her teaching career aside when their first child was born. Dad was the breadwinner.

Being an accomplished pianist and a trained teacher, Mama decided to teach piano lessons to make ends meet. This provided her some income during that year Dad was still with us, and it helped us survive those initial months right after he left.

God blessed Mama's efforts with a growing roster of children and satisfied parents. She was ready to plan her first student recital and arranged the venue to be at my elementary school for a Friday evening in June.

But there was a problem: the piano needed to be moved from the auditorium floor to the stage. The school administration told my mother she was responsible for having that done.

The day of the recital arrived full of sunshine. During our prayer time at breakfast, Mama asked the Lord to send some men to move that piano. We had heard that same petition many times over the past weeks.

Mama sat under the robust pine tree beside our front porch that afternoon. She took one of the two gingham dresses she had flung over her shoulder and began to hem it. I was proud to have a new yellow and white dress even though Anna would be wearing one just like it.

The task of hemming wouldn't take Mama long, but getting someone to move that piano would probably require frantic phone calls. The recital was just a few hours away, but Mama wasn't phoning anyone. As she stitched, she hummed "Amazing Grace," calm as ever.

I, however, was not calm. I was anxious. I wasn't worried about the piano getting moved but about performing in front of everyone. *What if I stumble on my way to the piano? What if I forget the notes? What if I can't stop my hands from shaking and hit the wrong keys?* I was terrified.

I thought about Mama's piano problem and how she didn't seem worried. I wondered if God could support me too—help me not be nervous. I whispered a prayer, asking God for strength, but I didn't tell anyone.

The afternoon Georgia heat seemed stifling as five-year-old Polly and I pressed against Mama's lawn chair. Polly had her favorite baby doll propped up on her shoulder, patting her back like a real baby. Mama's fingers flew through the stitches as she pulled each one to the rhythm of the song she hummed.

Suddenly, a gigantic black sedan with tinted windows pulled up to our mailbox. The sheer size of it frightened me. Four men, dressed in black as if to match their car, got out of the vehicle. I tightened my grip on the aluminum top of Mama's chair. My heart pounded double time. Trouble walked toward us in firm, measured strides like an army approaching its enemy.

I glanced at my mom to gauge her reaction. She was smiling at them; she wasn't afraid at all. I took my cue from her and gave them a welcoming grin as if they were the bearers of gifts and candy.

But the men did not return our smiles. After introducing themselves as the FBI, one of them pulled a document from his folder and showed it to my mother. The spokesman's words sounded flat, as if he were reading a phone book: "We have a warrant to search your house." The search warrant had something to do with my father and his business dealings before he left us.

Mama consented to these four giants entering our home. "Oh, and there is a basement, too," she called out after the screen door slammed behind them. She was as agreeable as if she were receiving a new washing machine.

After going through things in the house and basement, they came back outside to question Mama. By now, Anna and Rocky had joined us. We stood close to Mama like chicks around a mother hen. Mama answered each of their questions as one of them took notes. When there was a pause, she told the men we had to leave for a piano recital soon. She cheerfully added that she had not found any men who could move the piano for her.

As these men realized the living conditions of this thirtyish brunette, something must have happened in their hearts. Had they seen the depleted food storage? Had they noticed the few clothes in the closets? Did they stumble on the thread-bare carpets? Perhaps they realized this lady was earning grocery money for her family by teaching piano.

After glancing at the other men, the shortest one said, "Ma'am, we will follow you to the school and move that piano for you."

We all climbed into our turquoise chariot, so-called by Mama, because God had provided it for the gift price of only one dollar. A sweet couple who knew that Dad had taken our only car sold us their 1955 Ford. My mother's friend LaVelle explained that the vehicle drank a lot of oil, so he taught my nine-year-old brother to check the level and how to add more. I was proud of Rocky, who kept our old car fed with oil. This chariot also sported a small hole in the floorboard through which we could see the moving road beneath us. Mama assured us we were safe since she had put a rug over the hole. We didn't care what was wrong with the car; we were thankful it worked.

As Mama pulled our chariot onto the main road, I turned to see the ominous black sedan holding the four giants following behind us. While driving, Mama thanked God for sending the FBI men right when she needed them and for their kind hearts to help her. She prayed for their salvation and praised God for His faithfulness.

⟫⟫⟫  ⟪⟪⟪

"Amy, sweetheart," my mother whispered, "you're next."

I climbed the stage steps to the ebony piano, pulled out the scratched-up bench, and sat down. Since I had memorized "Für Elise," I didn't need to bring music. Resting my hands on the proper keys, I scanned the audience from my view on the stage. Mama was in the front row, beaming at me. She gave me the go-ahead nod.

I turned to the keyboard, took a deep breath, and began to play the song in my heart. I didn't perform like a nervous eleven-year-old but rather like the child of a faithful Father who was watching over me.

Whether the need is circumstantial, like for a piano to be moved for a recital, or if it is emotional, like a young child of God needing help to overcome her nervousness to perform in that recital, God delights when we ask Him for help and trust Him to answer!

⟫⟫⟫  ⟪⟪⟪

John 15:7: If you abide in me, and my words abide in you, ask whatever you wish, and it will be done for you.

# Chapter Seventeen

# Letting Go of My Treasures

**April 1966 (age 12) ~ Tucker, GA**

As I entered the store, my heart seemed to be running a fifty-yard dash. I opened my purple polka-dotted change purse and dug out coins to buy my latest treasure: the newest Trixie Belden book!

I felt grown up paying with my own money. I thanked the cashier as she handed me a brown bag that protected the book of adventures I would experience when I curled up on the sofa after we got home. Our family didn't have much money, but I could spend my birthday and Christmas money however I wanted. Another Trixie Belden book was at the top of my wish list.

About three years earlier, when I was nine, I had discovered this fiction series. I remember buying my very first book, *The Secret of the Mansion*, for fifty cents.

Trixie became my hero. She was similar to the famous fiction detective Nancy Drew, only better. Her bubbly personality and friendly banter drew me in. I learned new words from Trixie. In *The Secret of the Mansion*, I discovered the meaning of "sibling" when she referred to her brother. I felt proud to start using such an adult word.

Reading had become an escape for me. I could enter a different world than the one that was my current reality. I could help Trixie solve mysteries while sitting around a campfire. Perhaps the adults in my life would realize how brilliant I was, like the grown-ups in Trixie's life believed about her.

My stack of Trixie Belden books on the floor beside my bed became a tower. Every time a new one came out, I would save up for it.

Once, when I was in the hospital, my mother's friend JoAnn, whom I called Mama Dean, brought me *two* new Trixie Belden books. My hospital stay took a turn for the better that day. I now had all thirteen of the books that had been published up to that point, and contentment filled my body.

Then, a sorrowful day came. And my heart shattered into a thousand tiny pieces.

Mama heard about a girl my age, Ellie, who had been in a terrible car accident. She was in a body cast from her shoulders down to her hips, causing her to be confined to bed for a few months. My family prayed for her around the supper table during devotions.

Later, Mama entered my room, where I was reading against the closet door. She pushed some packing boxes aside and sat on Anna's bed. Once school finished, we would be moving to South Carolina to be closer to my grandparents. I thought Mama wanted to discuss our move. But that was not the case.

"Amy, do you remember the little girl we prayed for tonight who was in a car wreck?" she asked.

"Yes. Ellie, right?"

"That's right. I found out that her mother is searching for some good books for Ellie to read while she has to stay in bed. Maybe you could give her your Trixie Belden books. You have read them many times already. And giving them away would reduce the number of boxes when we move. I know she would love them. That would be such a kind thing to do. What do you think?" Her voice softened with her final question.

I wonder if she saw the light leave my eyes or if she heard my little gasp for air. I felt as if she had asked me to donate my eyes to a blind child.

My thoughts screamed inside my head: *Give them all away? And then move away, too?* That dashed any hope ever to get them back. But I said nothing out loud as I processed this life-altering suggestion.

I cherished my books so much that I wanted to save them to pass on to my daughters so they could experience the same joy these stories had given me. I studied Mama's soft expression and knew her idea was the right thing to do.

Sometimes, doing the right thing means giving up something loved to make another person happy. But that noble thought didn't cross my mind in this heavy moment.

All I could think about was losing something I treasured.

⤜⟫⟫⟫ ⟪⟪⟪⤛

I caressed the box on my lap as we drove to Ellie's house the next night. The moon looked like speckled cheese in the black sky, but my suffering prevented me from appreciating its beauty.

How would this poor girl receive my treasures? Would she rush through her schoolwork so she could get to reading again? Would she love the adventures as much as I did? Would Trixie become her hero too?

The tires crunched on the gravel driveway. The car door felt heavier than usual as I strained to push it open.

A petite woman with brown hair pulled into a ponytail greeted us at the door. She hugged us each awkwardly and then motioned for us to follow her down the hall to her daughter's bedroom.

Ellie's pink room was cozy, with stuffed animals everywhere. A TV was on a high shelf opposite her bed. A plastic doll house sat idle against one of the walls, with each little person frozen in their pretend activities.

I felt frozen too.

I wasn't sure how to have a conversation with this stranger. What should I say? "How are you?" would be a dumb question. "What did you do today?" wasn't much better. So I stood there holding the box while Mama started talking to Ellie.

"We are sorry about your accident, but we are thankful to Jesus for saving you and getting you good help." Mama often brought Jesus into conversations.

Mama motioned for me to come closer to the bed with the box. She continued, "Check these out, Ellie. These are Trixie Belden books that Amy has loved. We think you will like them too."

I reluctantly set the box of my beloved books on Ellie's bed with a smile that was more like a grimace. The reality of that night was I didn't give them willingly. And certainly not cheerfully.

I gave them because Mama wanted me to.

Fifteen years later

The Christmas tree was decorated in our home in Ghana, and carols played on the tape recorder. We were all excited for Christmas. My children, ages six, five, and almost four, clamored around me. "Mommy, is it time? Can we go now?"

"Do you each have the toy you want to give away?" I said as I pushed some hair out of Heidi's eyes and tucked it behind her ear.

They nodded enthusiastically, clutching the toy they had chosen from their treasures. They played almost daily with their Ghanaian friends who lived next door, and that is where we were headed.

We enjoyed instituting different Christmas traditions in our young family. This year, we started memorizing a scripture passage for our gift to Jesus. We were memorizing Luke 2:8–11. We continued to do this tradition through our children's entire childhoods.

We were implementing a shorter-lived tradition on this day. During the week before Christmas, our children each chose a toy to share with a friend. There was a critical guideline to choosing their toy to give away: it had to be something they treasured.

Years ago, my Trixie Belden books had comforted my young life. Those books had become more important to me than blessing someone in need. Even worse, I had depended on those books for security and satisfaction.

I now know that place belongs exclusively to God.

The screen door slammed as I followed my skipping children out the door.

I called out after them, "Let's go bless someone else with our treasures!"

⋙ ⋘

2 Corinthians 9:7: Each one must give as he has decided in his heart, not reluctantly or under compulsion, for God loves a cheerful giver.

# Chapter Eighteen

# Reaction to a Hate Prank

**Fall 1967 (age 14) ~ Columbia, SC**

I WAS FOURTEEN WHEN a hate prank against my mother helped to shape my faith.

The leaves had started to change colors; the fall chill was in the air. Mama had a closer-to-home job teaching high school English after commuting an hour away for our first few years in South Carolina.

On this Saturday morning, I woke up to the smell of bacon. We rarely had a special breakfast with bacon, so the scent drew me into the kitchen. I sat on a counter stool, watching Mama whisk up the eggs.

"Good morning, Glory," she greeted me with her favorite morning salutation.

Her pink quilted robe swished about her, making her appear like royalty to me, which she was. Her oversized front teeth formed a part of her perpetual smile. She even smiled when she sang.

"Thanks so much, sweetheart, for washing the dishes yesterday," Mama said.

When I got home from school, I had seen dirty dishes in the sink and cleaned them up. I seldom did the dishes on my own initiative, but on this day, I had. Maybe I was growing up. When Mama had arrived home from teaching, she saw the tidied-up kitchen and exclaimed, "Oh my! An angel came and washed our dishes!" I will never forget that. Such a simple act of service received such a powerful reaction.

Rocky and Polly joined us in the kitchen and sat down for breakfast.

The regular Saturday happenings got underway: laundry, dusting, homework, grading papers for Mama. My eight-year-old sister played dolls on the braided rug in the den while we "older folks" buzzed around doing chores. I missed Anna, who had moved in with my grandparents a month earlier because Mama had difficulty controlling her.

Suddenly, someone beeped in front of our house. We heard it several times as if the message was becoming more urgent. We all peered out the front screen door and saw a fire-engine red car full of teenage boys. Two of them were leaning out their windows, calling, "Mrs. Roth! Mrs. Roth!"

Mama dried her hands with the dish towel and threw it over the chair by the door. "Those are boys from my class who have come to see me!" She pushed open the screen and hurried down the cement steps toward their sporty Pontiac to talk with them.

When she was about half the distance from the front door to their vehicle, a dark-haired boy in the front seat drew his arm back and heaved something at her. Realizing the boy had thrown a firecracker, my brother shouted, "Mama, cover your eyes!"

The smell of burning rubber filled the air as the teens sped away with raucous laughter haunting my ears. Mama stumbled toward the front porch steps as we rushed to meet her. Rocky got on one side, and I the other. We wrapped our arms around her waist and guided her trembling body up the stairs. She uncovered her eyes and seemed unharmed—at least as okay as possible when a firecracker has been thrown at you.

*How can anyone do something so mean to another human, especially my kind mother?*

My heart pounded like a drum in my chest, partly from relief that Mama was not hurt and partly from anger at what those boys had done.

What happened next is forever seared in my memory: Mama went to the living room sofa, dropped to her knees, and began praying out loud for the salvation of those boys.

I wanted God to do something to them too, but it wasn't to save them!

Mama often prayed aloud, so we were used to this. Sometimes, she prayed with her head bowed, but other times she sought God's help with her face and eyes gazing up, like a young child looking up to her daddy for help.

This was a time like that—focusing on her Abba Father asking for mercy on her assailants and for their salvation.

I don't know what ever happened to any of those boys, but if God answered my mother's prayer for saving them, then I suspect she will hear some apologies in heaven.

No one likes to experience hateful injustices. As I reflect on my life, I remember my son's bike being stolen, my daughter being turned down for a job because of her skin color, a coworker misrepresenting me, and other heart-wrenching offenses.

But I thought of Mama on her knees as that car sped away, and I chose to do as she did.

I prayed for them.

Matthew 5:44: But I say to you, Love your enemies and pray for those who persecute you.

# Chapter Nineteen

# From Abandoned Daughter to Found Fiancée

**Fall 1972 (age 19) ~ Columbia, SC**

MY CHEST TIGHTENED WHEN I saw my girlfriend's dad playing checkers with her in the commons. I missed having a dad in my life. I drove home after classes, glad to be leaving the carefree banter of my friends who lived on campus.

A gentle breeze blew in my bedroom window. My first week of classes promised a stimulating semester. Now a sophomore at Columbia Bible College, I had decided to live at home and commute to school each day to save money. My scholarship covered most of my tuition but not room and board.

The clanging of pots in the kitchen jerked me out of my reflective state. "Hi, sweetheart," Mama greeted me as I entered the family room and sat on a counter stool.

After some small talk, I asked her, "Mama, do you miss Dad?" I still must have been in my reflective state. I didn't refer to my father as "daddy" because I believed that was an endearing term. He had lost the privilege of that title when he deserted us nine years earlier.

Mama cleared her throat and seemed to pull the words from the depths of her heart. "Oh yes, sweetheart. I miss him. I love him. I want him to return—first to God, then to me and our children."

"I miss him too. I miss having a man in my life who loves me," I said.

The beige phone hanging on the wall by the sink interrupted us with its shrill ring. My grandmother was calling. With elbows planted on the counter and hands cradling my face, I continued my reverie while waiting for their conversation to end.

I yearned for God to bring my father back or to let me meet the man I was going to marry—the man who would love me and whom I would love forever.

My mother pulled the long phone cord into the laundry room, lowering her voice. She must have needed privacy. I could take a hint. Feeling cut off from our deep conversation, I retreated to my bedroom.

My black-trimmed walnut desk, which I had purchased with babysitting money, held my open Bible. I slid into the vinyl-cushioned chair and fingered the delicate pages.

"Lord," I prayed, "I know You love me and have made me Your child. It's just that I miss having an earthly father who loves me. Would you please bring my dad back to You and to our family? Or would you bring me the man You have prepared for me to marry?"

In my prophets class, we were studying Isaiah. We learned how God delights in pouring out His grace on His people. The Israelites' unwillingness to listen to the prophets forced them to learn through affliction. God promised to guide those who put away their idols and followed Him instead.

Thinking of these truths, I opened to Isaiah 30 and read verse 18: "Therefore the Lord longs to be gracious to you, And therefore He waits on high to have compassion on you. For the Lord is a God of justice; How blessed are those who long for Him" (NASB).

Tears filled my eyes as the Lord's love covered me like a cozy fleece blanket. I continued to read, though the words were blurry now: "O people in Zion . . . you will weep no longer. He will surely be gracious to you at the sound of your cry; when He hears it, He will answer you" (NASB).

I realized that just like the Lord heard the children of Israel's cry, He was hearing mine too. I know now that I should have wanted my affections to belong to God alone more than the love of an earthly father or a boyfriend. He was the One who could satisfy me like no human because He is faithful. And His love is steadfast. But nineteen-year-old Amy wasn't there yet.

Instead, my desire was for God to answer my heartache by sending my father back or bringing my future husband into my life. I didn't know what the Almighty would do, but I knew He had heard my cry and cared about me.

❧ ❧

The following morning, warm sunrays filtered through my black-and-white houndstooth curtains. As I prepared for church, I committed my day to the Lord. The emotional struggles of the previous night were buried as the pressing needs of the morning took over my brain.

At church, I noticed a handsome young man barely clearing the doorway as he entered the vestibule. His blond hair had a part that appeared to have been made with a ruler. Later, I was introduced to this good-looking guy, Mark, and my heart was doing cartwheels.

That evening, after the service had ended, Mark stood alone outside, glancing around the parking lot. The vehicle that had brought him was gone. His roommate, John Crowe, had left the church with his car full of students but without Mark.

I gathered my courage and asked him if he needed a ride back to school. Our home was en route between the church and the college. I offered to give him a ride back to campus, but it would first involve an hour at my home for the high school/college kids' social time. Having no other way back to the dorm, he accepted.

Later, I found out what had brought Mark to this point. Here is what he shared:

I was led to Christ by a fellow student involved with the Navigator ministry at the University of Illinois. The Navigators discouraged dating and were known as the "never-daters." They taught us that godly guys didn't date. When I was a senior, I made a commitment to the Lord that I wouldn't date a girl again until I knew she was the one He had for me to marry.

The following fall, I began my year of training for missionary service at Columbia Graduate School. I was assigned to a small Bible church with my roommate, John, who drove me and others to the Sunday services because he had a car on campus. After the evening service that first week, my roommate unknowingly drove back to campus without me.

I was standing in front of the church wondering what I would do when a girl saw my confusion and invited me to what the church called "Afterglow"—a time of fellowship for young people hosted at her home that night.

Having no other way back to the dorm, I accepted. I soon met Amy's godly mother, family, and other church youth. Afterward, Amy drove me back to campus.

⟿ ⟾

Driving in pouring rain as we returned to campus that evening, we noticed a vehicle in a steep ditch, taillights still glowing. We parked in the grass behind them, keeping our headlights on to give us light. The female driver was semi-conscious but seemed uninjured as she lay slumped over the wheel. Two crying kids were clinging to each other in the back seat. I brought the children into my car while Mark tried to assist the driver. She regained consciousness quickly, but Mark couldn't understand her slurred words. Once she was resting in the front seat, Mark tried to figure out how to pull the car out of the ditch.

Seven-year-old Sabrina and three-year-old Dwayne calmed down as I spoke gently to them, letting them know they were safe. Once the hiccupy cries stopped, they answered my questions about their lives and interests. Turning the conversation to spiritual things, I shared with Sabrina about sins I had committed as a child. Her eyes grew big, and she said, "I've done that too." I told her how Jesus died for my sins so I could be forgiven and become His child. I quoted John 1:12: "But as many as received Him, to them He gave the right to become children of God, even to those who believe in His name" (NASB).

"Did Jesus die for my sins too?" Sabrina asked. God's Holy Spirit worked in her heart; she trusted Him as her Savior that night.

We called the police from a neighbor's home because we couldn't get the vehicle out of the ditch. Mark and I didn't want to leave the young family without help. Once the police arrived, we got the family's name and address from the woman who had awakened from her drunken state and was able to converse.

The next day, when I ran into Mark on the sidewalk between the two dorms, we had the same idea: we wanted to follow up with this family, especially since Sabrina had become a believer. The address led to an ethnic area of town I had never visited. We couldn't find the driver but Sabrina and Dwayne were glad to see us and gave me a bear hug.

Over the next several months, we ran a Bible club ministry with ten to fifteen children and preteens from their neighborhood. I taught the children Bible truths, verses, and songs while Mark played with the two- and three-year-olds.

Mark's roommate noted how much time Mark and I were spending together. He pointed this out to Mark in an older brother, protective way. John also embraced the never-daters' philosophy. Mark responded: "You don't need to worry. I'm not interested in that way."

We continued our investment in these kids' lives and rejoiced when some came to know the Lord. Our hearts for reaching others with the gospel were the same: it was a burning passion more important than romance. Even so, my insides vibrated whenever I knew I was going with Mark to teach the children. God used that ministry time to spark that initial flame of attraction in His creative plan for us.

After several weeks of our outreach together, when the auburn leaves were letting go from the trees, Mark told John, "You better start worrying."

He was falling for me!

Mark finished his one-year Bible certificate in the spring. We continued our courtship through letters. In the late fall of 1973, during my junior year, Mark sent me tickets to visit his family in the Chicago area for Christmas.

Exiting O'Hare's sliding doors, Mark led me to his parked Ford. Once inside, we communicated our feelings with our eyes and then embraced to melt away the months we had been apart. Our growing affection was like a symphony—full of booming crescendos and soft interludes. Mark's love for me was music to my soul.

One snowy, windy day, we walked together on Greenwood Avenue, where he grew up. I felt cozy inside my white polar bear coat Mama had given me for an early Christmas present. As we strolled hand in hand, I said, "Isn't it something how both of us are from solid Christian homes?" Then I stopped abruptly, bewildered at what I had said. "Oh wait, my parents are separated. My father left our family. He doesn't follow Jesus." I stood there on the freshly shoveled sidewalk, trying to summarize the spiritual atmosphere of my childhood in my mind.

With deliberate words, I continued, "But I *feel* like I am from a solid Christian upbringing because of how my mom taught us about the Lord."

God gave me security in my mother's love and commitment to Him. Because she raised us to know and follow our Heavenly Father, I forgot momentarily that my dad wasn't in the picture.

I believe God brought good out of my dad deserting our family because it put me in a home centered on obeying and serving Jesus, albeit with only one parent.

Most people shake their heads when they hear my childhood stories. They say, "That's so sad." But I don't think of my childhood that way.

Looking in life's rearview mirror, I see how God brought good from every trial—even the desertion of my dad.

Romans 8:28: And we know that for those who love God all things work together for good, for those who are called according to his purpose.

We got married in a garden in Addis Ababa Ethiopia.
1975 (left) First family photo. 1976 (right)

Teaching young women in the Bible School in Waka. 1976.
(above) Benjy helps roll a barrel in Kumasi. 1978 (below)

Getting ready to start our 3 day trek to Yeli (left) in 1976. On our trek out to Soddo for more supplies (right).

That small white image in the center is an MAF plane landing our airstrip in Waka in 1976.

Family photo in summer of 1959 (left). Easter 1960 after
Polly joined us in Dec. 1959 (right).

I don't have very many photos of me as a child, but
here are a few: 13 months, 3 yrs, 6 yrs, 15 yrs.

Mother/daughter matching dresses. 1981 (left).
Harvesting bananas in our Kumasi yard. 1985 (right).

Deeanne & Heidi show their cross-stitched pillows from me
at ICA. 1987 (left) Benjy hops on our friend's motorcycle for
a picture in Kumasi. 1982 (right)

Kinza's adoption day in Tamale 1993 (left). Colette listening to a Bible story. 1996 (right).

Family together for the summer in State College, PA. 1996

Ben graduated from ICA in 1994. (left) Heidi graduated in 1997. (right) Deeanne graduated in 1996. (below)

My father (left) died in July 2008. His brother, Stefan, came from California for the service. Uncle Stefan is pictured below with me and my siblings. From left to right: Stefan, Anna, Amy, Rocky, and Polly.

Mama (right) died in April 2014 in Jonesboro, GA. Mark and I are pictured below with our children at her funeral. From left to right: Heidi, Kinza, Mark, Amy, Ben, Deeanne, and Colette.

# Section IV

# God's Plan in my Spiritual Formation

# Chapter Twenty

# Childhood Threads Woven for God's Purposes

**July 1953 ~ Columbia, SC**

WHILE MAMA LABORED AT the hospital waiting for my arrival, my dad was at a Cincinnati Reds baseball game with some friends. At that time, it was uncommon for the father to be in the delivery room. But usually he was in a nearby waiting room, also known as the Stork Club, eagerly awaiting word of his newborn baby. Not my dad. He seemed to be eagerly awaiting the next home run.

My parents had welcomed a girl, Anna, two years earlier. Now, baby number two was about to be born.

During the baseball game, my dad called the maternity ward to see if his wife had delivered. He identified himself as George Roth, but the nurse mistakenly heard "Ross," the surname of another new mother on the ward.

"Oh yes, Mr. Ross, you have a son!" the nurse said.

As my mother told me the account of my birth, she said, "Your dad was overjoyed about having a boy, and he gave out blue-banded cigars to his friends. Later when he got to the hospital, he told me he was thrilled about having a son. I was surprised to realize his misunderstanding, but I quickly corrected him. 'Oh, she is not a boy; she is a girl! And she is beautiful. Go see her.'"

Perhaps this was the first strike against my relationship with him: his disappointment that I was not a boy.

Three years earlier, my mother was encouraged by her future mother-in-law to attend the Billy Graham Crusade at the Columbia Township Auditorium. In Mama's testimony years later, she wrote:

> If anyone was born "religious," I was. Even as a youth, I was very active in church, teaching younger girls and singing in the choir. But I never could be "good enough." Such striving on my part led to an emotional breakdown, so my senior year in college was scaled back to the minimum hours needed to graduate. When George's mother, Pauline, invited me to an evangelistic crusade, I steeled myself against something I believed was out of my league. The words "sin" and "saved" were foreign to me. But when Pauline came home radiant with the joy of the Lord from the Spirit-empowered meeting, I couldn't resist anymore. The following week, I attended and sang with the choir. I heard Billy Graham's sermon on Revelation 3:20 and went forward to receive Christ as my Savior on March 2, 1950.

Once my mother trusted Jesus as her Lord and Savior, she devoured His Word. Attending church fed her soul and made her hungry for more. She constantly searched the radio for sermons. In addition to the Bible, she read missionary biographies to help her grow in her ability to witness about her newfound faith.

One of her favorite books was about Amy Carmichael, a missionary to India. Reading this biography intrigued her, and it was her first introduction to missions. She learned about Carmichael's ministry while she was pregnant with me.

Mama's due date for my birth was July 7, the birthday of my paternal grandfather, Amasa Boyd Roth. His mother nicknamed him Amsie. Desiring the honor of a grandson named after him, he generously offered to pay for my college education if my parents gave their son his name.

My mother prayed that God would give her another daughter. I don't know if she wanted a girl to avoid a son named Amasa. She didn't tell me why she wanted a girl. After I was born, Mama asked her father-in-law if "Amy" would be close enough to his name. My grandfather said yes. Although he didn't pay for my college tuition, he paid for the hospital bill, a welcomed gift for my parents.

And just like that, Amasa Boyd, named after his grandfather, became Amy Elisabeth, named after a missionary and in honor of her grandfather.

That would be me.

Mama's love for knowing God's Word was engraved into my childhood memories. While she ironed, she played a record of scripture being read in the King James version. I can still hear the man's deep voice repeating the refrain in Psalm 136: "For his mercy endureth for ever." At first, I thought the record was stuck, but I eventually figured out that the phrase was repeated over and over in that Psalm. When we played outside, she sat in her lawn chair with her Bible on her lap. While driving, she asked me to check her as she recited a chapter she had memorized.

She was also passionate about telling others about Jesus. We kids would avoid eye contact with the gas attendant at her driver's window while she asked him if he knew her Jesus. The tract she held ready in her hand soon was in the attendant's possession, who was nodding his head.

When I was six, she invited a lady from church to our house. JoAnn was tall, with short red hair and a worried face. Luckily for me and my brother, she brought along her two kids, Charlotte and Mallory, who were our ages.

We noticed our mothers kneeling in front of the sofa when we ran through the den during our play. My mother led JoAnn to the Lord that day. They began studying God's Word and praying together every week. The four of us kids became friends for life.

My mother longed to support a missionary—to send some money to help reach the world with the gospel. My dad told her no: we didn't have money for that.

Once she started teaching piano lessons, she sent some of her earnings to SIM to support Dr. Ian Hay. She had heard him share about his ministry in Ethiopia and wanted to help.

She had no idea that approximately twelve years later, her second-born daughter would be a missionary with that same mission in the same country where Dr. Hay had served.

After the dust settled following my father's desertion, my mother acted on her desire to serve the Lord overseas. As the boss of our family now, she applied to teach at Faith Academy, a missionary kids' school in the Philippines. In God's plan, she was rejected by the mission board. As she relayed the story to me, with a twinkle in her eye, she said, "But God told me not to worry—He would send one of my children to the foreign mission field."

God fulfilled His promise to her by sending me to Ethiopia for three years and Ghana for twenty years. He allowed her the joy of visiting us once in Ethiopia and twice in Ghana, where she experienced sharing Jesus in another culture alongside her missionary daughter.

March 2005

Once we were reunited with my father, we visited him and his wife, Ginny, every few years in New Orleans when our travels took us south. Although my father did not follow the Lord, he had grown up with a godly mother who took him to church and taught him about God's love.

During one of our visits, Dad shared a story from his childhood with me. When my dad turned nine on February 5, 1938, his mother took him to an evangelistic meeting to hear Reverend Charles Taylor. Afterward, she told Reverend Taylor it was her son's birthday—a birthday shared with Dwight L. Moody. She asked Reverend Taylor to pray a blessing for her son. Reverend Taylor put his hand on my father's head and prayed for him.

As my father concluded this story, he said, "I believe you, Amy, are God's answer to his prayer."

July 2007

On my fifty-fourth birthday, Mama gave me a copy of Elisabeth Elliot's biography of Amy Carmichael. Here is the inscription Mama wrote on the title page to me:

This book is about the Amy for whom you are named—but how little did I know in 1953—that

Amy Carmichael and Amy Roth would have so much in common in their lives of service and utter devotion to our Lord Jesus! Amy Carmichael in her way as a single woman who mothered many in the 19th/20th century(ies) that she lived—and Amy Roth Hagerup as a married mother who has discipled many in the 20th/21st century(ies)—and still is! With all my love & admiration, Mama

Reading Mama's comparison clarifies what rose-colored glasses a mother wears for her offspring. I am far beneath the spiritual stature of selfless Amy Carmichael. But I serve the same God Amy served, and He is the only One who is worthy of praise.

The desire God put in my mother's heart to be a foreign missionary was fulfilled in Him using her to raise me to love Him and His Word and to want to share the gospel at home and abroad.

God can use the circumstances of one generation to bring about His purposes for the next generation.

Psalm 37:4: Delight yourself in the Lord, and he will give you the desires of your heart.

# Chapter Twenty-One

# A Longing to Belong

**June 1963 (age 9) ~ Tucker, GA**

I LOOKED AROUND THE choir room with my heart racing, trying to find Mama. The church was enormous, and I often felt alone.

"No, little girl. It would be best if you left now. You don't belong here." The kind-hearted lady wearing beige grandma shoes guided me toward the door. "Go back to the nursery and play with the children until choir practice ends."

The plinking of piano keys filtered through the living room door where Mama was giving a lesson. *Lucky girl—she has my mother all to herself.* Quietly, I turned the doorknob and cracked open the door to peek into the room. Mama turned on her stool while keeping her pencil on the sheet music. "Please close the door, sweetheart. You know you don't belong here while I am teaching."

I sat on the back steps, arms wrapped around my knees, hugging myself. I heard my older sister playing with our neighbors, and my younger brother, Rocky, tinkering on his bike with his friend. I certainly didn't belong with them.

"I can't wait to go to camp next month with Charlotte." Talking to myself brought me comfort during these lonely times. I day-dreamed about the experiences I would be having at a weeklong, spend-the-night party with other girls in my cabin.

We were going to camp the week after my tenth birthday.

Charlotte and I walked down the center aisle of the giant green tent at Camp Cameron, kicking the sawdust as we went. We were early to claim seats in the folding wooden chairs for the evening meeting. The smell of pines all around us was a constant reminder that we were in the middle of a forest. Our brothers, Mallory and Rocky, were there too, which took away some of the scariness of being far from home.

A generous couple from our church had paid the way for Rocky and me to attend for the week. I realized going to camp was a treat—an experience that our parents could not afford to give us.

Camp days were filled with swimming, making crafts, and hiking in the woods. But the thing I loved the most was mealtime: pork and beans, mac and cheese, hamburgers, banana pudding. And I could eat all my little heart (or stomach!) desired. I never went to bed hungry while at camp.

Spiritual truths were presented daily on a level I could grasp. I heard how we are all sinners, which I already knew, but somehow, this fact hit me harder this week—as in, "I, Amy, am a sinner."

On the second night, I leaned forward on my wooden chair, causing the back legs to come off the ground. The preacher was talking directly to me. My heart had an itchy feeling—a "longing" kind of sensation. I wanted this—no, I needed this—this Jesus who loves me. When the invitation was given, I gave Charlotte a side glance to say, "I'm going up." I stood up and headed to the front, where the preacher was leaning down to talk to another camper already there.

A female counselor dressed in a lime-green shift dress with a matching scarf put her arm around me and led me to an empty seat in the front row. She spoke gently to me—her words felt like how love must sound. Miss Shirley opened her Bible to Romans 3:23 and asked me to read that verse. "For all have sinned and fall short of the glory of God." I didn't need convincing of my sin: disobedience. Wanting to be first in line. Grabbing the last piece of cake. Being unkind to Rocky or Polly. Telling lies. All of these and more characterized my young life. I knew I was a sinner who needed Jesus to save me.

Miss Shirley then flipped a few pages over to Romans 6:23 and again asked me to read it: "For the wages of sin is death, but the free gift of God is eternal life through Christ Jesus our Lord." I knew Romans 6:23 because Mama had taught us a lot of verses. I nodded that I understood.

I remember the delighted expression on Miss Shirley's face. "And now the good news, Amy. Let's find Romans 10:9. See what it says." She pointed with her slender finger and read: "If you confess with your mouth that Jesus is Lord and believe in your heart that God raised Him from the dead, you will be saved."

"What do you think 'confess with your mouth' means?" she asked.

I pondered for a minute because I didn't want to give the wrong answer and appear stupid. "Does it mean to say it out loud?"

"Yes! That's right. And what does 'believe in your heart' mean?" She continued to check my understanding.

Now, I felt bolder. "I think it means to believe something—not just like a fact in your head, but believing deep down here," I said as I thumped my chest with my fist.

"You have good insights, Amy. You got it exactly right. Would you like to do that?"

Her words were like a balm to my hurting insides. "Yes. I would."

On July 9, 1963, with the musty smell of sawdust on the floor, I asked Jesus to forgive my sins, thanked Him for dying on the cross and rising again, and invited Him to be my Lord and Savior.

I became a child of God.

When I lifted my head from praying, my counselor whispered my name, "Amy?" My questioning blue eyes met her confident brown ones.

"Now you belong to Jesus. And Jesus belongs to you."

Luke 18:16: But Jesus called for them, saying, "Permit the children to come to Me, and do not hinder them, for the kingdom of God belongs to such as these.

# Chapter Twenty-Two

# When Rose-colored Glasses Were a Good Thing

**Spring 1970 (age 16) ~ Columbia, SC**

AFTER HEARING "CHARGE," I stepped forward from the line of Bible-holding teens standing at the front of the church. "Hebrews 13:8. Jesus Christ is the same yesterday and today and forever," I said while my friends flipped pages to find the verse.

"That is correct," the moderator announced, and the scorekeeper added those points to my name. I stepped back into the line of sword drill contestants to wait for the next reference while Mama beamed.

Augusta Street Church in West Columbia did not have a large congregation—less than one hundred adults. But what it lacked in numbers, it made up in care and compassion.

When we first moved to South Carolina, my mother's friends told her about this church. They also must have told the church about our family because something curious happened after our first Sunday evening service. We pulled into our driveway on a dead-end street that hardly saw any traffic except for us and our next-door neighbors. My brother said, "Hey, look. There's a car behind us. And another one after that. And another one. And they are all parking! What's going on?"

It turned out that they were giving us a "pounding." My mother laughed while telling us about this southern tradition of welcoming newcomers. Our new church family brought us food: a pound of this and a pound of that. They filled our cupboards with flour, sugar, and canned goods and our fridge with milk, eggs, and butter. We were the recipients of a pounding.

They filled our hearts, too, with the loving care of a new church family.

Over the next few years, I realized Augusta Street Church was mission-minded. Missionary speakers gave their presentations regularly. I entered their worlds through slide presentations about their ministry to share the gospel, translate the Bible, or work in medical missions. The lesson taught during each conference was that there were three ways to be involved: praying, giving, and going. So far, I had participated in the first two. I was hopeful that someday God would send me overseas, too.

One spring, when I was sixteen, my church planned a sword drill for the youth group. In a sword drill, the moderator calls out a scripture reference, and then the participants try to find it. The first one to locate it steps forward and reads it. If a person knows the scripture by memory, he or she can step forward and recite it.

Our pastor and youth leader wanted to encourage young people to know God's Word and navigate the Bible efficiently. The two high scorers of the sword drill would win a two-week mission trip to Haiti, where they would visit missionaries and learn about cross-cultural ministry. *What an exciting prize!*

I was thrilled when I won the sword drill, and my brother, Rocky, came in second place. My desire to experience life as a missionary in a different country was coming true.

Arriving in Port au Prince, we heard a voice call out to us: "Over here." A fortyish man with ash-blond hair stood amid teens who had arrived from another church for the mission trip. We felt an immediate bond as if our favorite uncle and cousins had come to pick us up, even though they were all strangers.

After hugs and back slaps, we claimed our luggage and followed the seasoned missionary out the main door. The heat hit me like opening the oven door to put in my aunt's yeast rolls. Sweat started to form along my hairline even before we reached the van. But nothing could wilt the blossoming in my heart to learn about being a missionary in another country.

The locally hired van bumped along the dirt road as we traveled to two missionary homes built an acre apart on a hill. The guys were led to a barn-type building where they would sleep, so Rocky went there. We girls were housed with the missionaries' teenage daughters in their bedrooms. Sleeping bags claimed all the available floor space.

After a few days of orientation and simple language learning, we were taken to a nearby village to immerse in the culture for a few days. The mode of transport for this outing was not a van or motorcycle, which the missionaries frequently used, but mules. Clomping along as if he had until Christmas to get there, my mule gave me no worries about being thrown. If I had dismounted and walked alongside him, I would have gotten there sooner with fewer thigh muscles complaining.

But I didn't complain: I was living a missionary life.

Little girls in their school uniforms of white shirts and royal blue skirts surrounded us as our mules entered the village. I gazed into their dark, innocent eyes, watching me fight with my skirt as I dismounted.

Despite the language barrier, I felt enveloped by love and respect as we gathered at tables to eat supper. Ladies who had labored over large pots on open fires served us generous portions. We had a stew of legumes and vegetables served over a rice pyramid. My tastebuds did a happy dance as I ate.

On Sunday morning, after a breakfast of plantain porridge, we hiked the dusty path on the south side of the village to the mud hut church. The trail narrowed as we got closer, and we had to step into the bushes several times to let others pass. The sound of macaws calling to each other reminded me of God's creativity here in Haiti.

Best of all was the joy I felt as children squeezed beside me on the path, clinging to my hands. Other little brown hands held onto my dress from behind as if the connection was necessary to claim a right to me. I felt like a queen ant carried by smaller ants to her destination.

Inside the church, there were rows of low benches; I sank gratefully onto one. My little friends sat beside me—all in a fluid motion as if they were one instead of eight. I grinned at their determination to be near me, fully aware I didn't deserve such attention.

The service opened with a Haitian elder welcoming the congregation and praying. The morning sun streamed through the windows, their shutters propped open with sticks. I thought of how the same sun shines into church windows worldwide—whether propped-open ones in Haiti or stained-glass ones in Rome.

The missionary up front nodded to Rocky and me, indicating it was time for our duet. During our first few nights at the missionary compound, we had learned the Creole words to a song we knew. I stood at the front beside my brother, my hands trembling. *Can we do this? Will I remember the words?* Worrisome thoughts scampered through my mind. I prayed silently for help.

"*Mwen pa poukont mwen ...*" We began singing "I'm Not Alone" in unknown-to-us words, though the tune was etched deep in my soul. We harmonized as I thought about the meaning of each word since I knew them in English. The song spoke of not being alone and having a friend, Jesus, who walks beside us.

When the final note was sung, my brother and I glanced at each other, sharing a connection through our eyes before returning to the benches. Sitting down, my mind flashed back to a few days earlier when I had walked over to where Rocky was staying. He had not been well and was resting in his bunk while the others were out on an assignment. The door was open to let the breeze come through the room.

What I saw made me drop the towels I was carrying. Rocky lay unconscious with his eyes open; I thought he had died. Rushing to his side, I shook him while shooing flies away from his face. He closed his eyes and made a sighing sound. "Thank You, Jesus," I said as the blood rushed back to my extremities. *He wasn't dead after all.* (I found out later Rocky had suffered a heat stroke.)

With a jolt, I returned to the present church service. A timid girl who was about four years old stood before me with her hands on my knees. Her pleading eyes seemed to say, "Please love me." I pulled her onto my lap and snuggled my cheek against hers. I have learned that a gentle human touch is needed to nurture a child's heart.

We listened to the pastor expounding God's Word from the makeshift pulpit. Neither of us understood much—I in my lack of knowledge of Creole and she in her youth. The service ended, and warm greetings were shared with us visitors as we filed out. There is no language barrier when it comes to smiles and tone of voice.

The following day, the blue sky was punctuated by white puffs of clouds outlined by darker ones. I was hopeful the rain would hold off during our mule ride back to the mission compound. After another breakfast of steaming porridge, I lugged my sleeping bag and overnight tote over to the other teens packing up while avoiding the chickens darting across the path.

My self-appointed three-foot-high welcome committee was back as the send-off committee. I knelt to hug each one individually. Amid giggles and mostly futile boosts up onto my mule from my send-off committee, I found myself in the saddle again, which was still as hard as a tortoise shell. I examined the faces of these precious children—each made in the image of God—and tried to communicate God's love and care for them through my countenance.

A minuscule slice of our lives intersected briefly. Those children probably forgot about me by the following week or even the next day. But their impact on my life was far more significant than an entry in my journal.

God used these loving children to communicate to my heart the path He had for me in sharing His love on the foreign mission field. They represented children worldwide pleading with their eyes as if to ask, "Who will tell us about your Jesus so we can know Him too?" I adjusted my rose-colored glasses.

I responded in my heart: "Here am I, Lord. Send me."

⤙⥲⥲⥲⥲⥲ ⥶⥶⥶⥶⥶⤚

Short-term mission trips are like that—rose-colored glasses are worn the entire time. But reality quickly becomes apparent when someone gets down in the trenches of overseas missionary life. Languages are difficult to learn. Local food can be hard to stomach. Customs take time to figure out and even longer to understand. Children are not gazing into the missionary's eyes, wanting to hear about Jesus.

Once I arrived in Ethiopia, it didn't take long to lose the rose-colored glasses I had worn for foreign missions. They weren't needed anyway.

But I never lost my glasses for the gift of a loving local church during my teen years. Those glasses were clear—not rose-colored—because I saw and experienced a devoted body of believers investing in my spiritual growth and being a crucial part of God directing me into missions.

1 Corinthians 12:24–25: But God has so composed the body . . . that the members may have the same care for one another.

# Section V

# God's Presence in my Children's Lives

# House Arrest with Our Baby

**April 1977 ~ Waka, Ethiopia**

WHILE TAKING THE LAST diaper off the clothesline, I heard shouting down the path, which sounded like it was coming from the school. Our mission compound was perched on flat land surrounded by steep valleys and mountains. It consisted of an elementary school, a Bible school and dorms, a clinic, teachers' dwellings, and two missionary homes. Waka was not accessible by car, but a single-engine airplane could land on a narrow strip of land between two steep valleys. Knowing the caliber of the Bible students, I dismissed the possibility of a disturbance.

I opened the screen door, turning sideways to fit through with the clothes basket. Benjy toddled up to me as fast as his wobbly legs would go. "Hi, sweetheart. Mommy needs to go lie down." I was thrilled to be expecting baby number two but was weakened by morning sickness. Nausea was part of the whole pregnancy package—a small price to pay for the gift of another child.

Mark took the basket from me. "Go rest for a while. I will bring you some crackers." With a gentle hand on my back, he pointed me toward the bedroom. I mentioned that something seemed to be happening at the Bible school, but the noise had quieted down. I crawled on top of the brown and orange patchwork bedspread as my stomach churned.

The bedroom walls felt like they were closing in on me. The double bed barely fit in the room—similar in size to a trailer bedroom. While lying there, I heard voices in the living room and realized we had visitors. Mark was conversing in Amharic with some men.

Suddenly, the bedroom door swung open, and a line of soldiers in uniform trooped into my private space. They gathered around the three sides of our bed, the only standing room available. I sat up, startled. Mark was at the end of the line holding Benjy.

"What's happening?" I wasn't sure if this was a nightmare or real life.

"Don't be afraid, Amy. These men need to talk to us. Can you get up now?" Mark asked.

As intimidating as it was to have these soldiers surrounding my bed, I said, "Sure." I can't remember how many soldiers there were—six or eight. They had guns but were not aiming them at me or Mark.

I followed the entourage back into the living room and put water on the stove to boil for tea while the men settled themselves on our sofa and chairs. Using my left hand to steady my trembling right one, I poured the tea. My prayer was simple: "Help, Lord!"

As I served the tea, I watched my fifteen-month-old son engaging with the soldiers. Benjy didn't see this as an anxiety-producing visit. He cheerfully brought each man one of his toys, which they accepted. One of them put his army hat on Benjy's head and our son erupted in giggles when the hat fell over his eyes. Benjy was interacting with the soldiers as if they were his long-lost uncles. Our armed visitors seemed touched, and I noticed warm smiles and a softer approach.

The men told us we were being investigated and put under house arrest until they decided how to proceed. We were informed that we could not sell our belongings and that any travel would require their permission.

The Ethiopian church leaders used a storage shed outside our house as a private office. The soldiers sealed that up by gluing paper from the door frame to the wood door with their signatures on the document. If the seal was broken, they would know the room had been entered without their approval. The army wanted control of the church, too.

The fate of our Bible school students was much worse than our house arrest. Mark accompanied the soldiers to the school after they finished with us. The authorities assembled the students, threatened them, and ordered them to return to their homes within four days or be arrested.

That evening, during our mission's two-way radio session, we learned that six other SIM stations had been visited that day, and those missionaries put under house arrest too. The new government restrictions were happening all over the country. I didn't fear for my life but was concerned for my son and my unborn baby. I needed to trust God with my children in this trial.

A few days later our mission sent veteran mission leader Merle Dye to Waka to assist us. Mark and the church leaders sought the necessary permission of the army and the governor for Merle to land on the airstrip near our house. On the day of his arrival, armed men and authorities gathered to meet him with an expectation of hostility. When Merle with the MAF pilot approached the men, he was friendly and direct. His humble demeanor disarmed them as Benjy had done the week before. They also realized we were friends of Ethiopia, not enemies. On the spot, they lifted the house arrest order and restored our complete freedom.

Even though we were no longer under house arrest, this was the beginning of our departure from Waka after a short nine-month assignment there. With the unrest in the country growing, it was no longer wise to remain at an isolated post.

Thinking back on what happened, I stand in wonder that God not only used a seasoned, older missionary to diffuse this hostile situation, but He also used our little son. Age or experience aren't the qualifiers for being able to be used by God.

God can use whomever He chooses to accomplish His good purposes—no matter the age.

Exodus 4:11–12: Then the Lord said to him, "Who has made man's mouth? Who makes him mute, or deaf, or seeing, or blind? Is it not I, the Lord? Now therefore go, and I will be with your mouth and teach you what you shall speak."

# Chapter Twenty-Four

# A School Choice Dilemma

**Fall 1982 ~ Arlington Heights, IL**

I GENTLY CLOSED THE memoir *Letters I Never Wrote* with tears tiptoeing down my cheeks. I hurt for the author, who had been sent off to boarding school at six years old. I ached for her parents who made such a personal sacrifice to allow their child to be educated away from them. Not knowing their situation, I inwardly judged them for their actions. How could anyone allow their child to go to boarding school? Not me, that's for sure.

October 1984 ~ Kumasi, Ghana

"Get out your math workbooks and turn to the next lesson," I said. My three elementary children settled into their places around the dining room table while the ceiling fan stirred the toasty African air. They attended a British international school daily from eight a.m. until twelve thirty, which gave me the afternoons to teach them American subjects.

Ridge International School in Kumasi only went through class five, the U.S. equivalent of fourth grade. Once our oldest finished at Ridge, we would need another school choice. Although we were incorporating homeschooling into their education, we all (both kids and parents) agreed that homeschooling full time after finishing at Ridge wasn't for our family. Returning to the United States was an option, but we did not have peace about that either.

We investigated school options for our children. The first stages weren't that stressful—praying, researching, and visiting schools. Interviews with teachers, parents, and students went well and we continued to seek the Lord's direction for us. The possibility of boarding school loomed before me. I secretly hoped that would not be God's good will for our family.

My head knew all the positives of boarding school for our kids, but my heart selfishly said no. I desired to hang onto our children. I wanted to be the primary influence in their young lives—the one teaching them, tucking them into bed, and hearing about their days. I asked the Lord to remove the "cup" of boarding school from me. Then I added, "But not my will, but Yours be done."

Lying in bed, troubled thoughts claimed real estate in my brain. Was I willing to allow our children to go to boarding school? I shifted my weight, turned to the other side, and sought a cool spot on the bedsheet. Sleep alluded me. Sometimes, I desire God's will wholeheartedly, but I inwardly hope and pray that His will aligns with mine.

A visit to Ivory Coast Academy (ICA) excited our kids for this schooling option. Classroom projects, dramas and musicals, sports, and lots of children to play with were benefits they wanted. If we decided on this plan, they would start in Berea Dorm, which was set up family style with first through eighth graders—a wing for boys down one side and girls down the other. The dorm parents included a married couple and a single lady.

Everything came together to show us that this was God's plan for our family, starting with our two oldest for the next school year there. Space opened up in the dorm, finances were provided, and our children were eager and ready. Most importantly, God gave us peace to move forward. I changed my prayer from "Please remove this cup" to "Show me this plan is good for us and our kids."

Sewing on name tags, packing up suitcases, preparing special cross-stitched pillows, and writing fun letters to be given by the dorm parents to each child weekly—the preparations seemed endless.

Finally, D-day arrived in August 1986. Our family packed up our double-cab pickup truck for the ten-hour excursion to Boauké. Five passports were tucked safely into my handbag, and we set out on this life-altering trip. We would be entrusting our fifth-grade son and third-grade daughter to other "called-by-God" adults for their training and nurturing. It would be six long weeks until our first visit.

Once at the school, we were given their room assignments and shown to their rooms. Our son's roommate wasn't there yet, so Benjy and I were alone in his room. "Mom, I think I see Steve outside. I'll be back in a minute." And with that, I was left alone in his cell—I mean, dorm room—holding his shorts with his name tag sewn neatly on the waistband. I stroked the name tag with my thumb. Benjy Hagerup. My son. My only son. This pair of shorts belonged to my son. And my son belonged to me. But did he really belong to me?

I glanced out the window and saw a cluster of boys riding their bikes down the dirt road in front of Berea. I was reminded that no, he didn't belong to me. He was on loan to me from God—entrusted to me for a season to teach and to oversee experiences allowed so God could do His ultimate work in him.

I returned to the task and placed the shorts in his drawer. Suddenly, my hand began to tremble, and I felt like I would lose my lunch. I collapsed onto the edge of his bed and took deep breaths. What was I doing putting my son's clothes in these drawers 350 miles from home? I had an urge to put his clothes back into the suitcase and slam it shut.

"Father, You promised!"

And the peace that passes any human comprehension flooded my heart. Peace. Only God.

Heidi, starting third grade, joined her ICA siblings the following school year. Now, they were sixth, fourth, and third graders. Deep breath. Was the first semester of our second year at Ivory Coast Academy almost over? I studied the wall calendar and counted the days until my husband would go to get our precious cherubs.

I gingerly picked up their most recent letters and reread them. I bowed my head to pray, but my mind seemed stuck on "what if?" scenarios. Worry does that to me, making me forget what God has promised. I wanted to take control, especially when it involved our children. And I was bombarded with "what ifs?"

What if my children were being bullied and didn't know who to tell?

What if Heidi was crying herself to sleep at night?

What if they said they were doing okay, but deep down they were struggling?

*How can I know, Lord? Help me to trust You.*

I inhaled the warm evening air, filling my lungs with the peace He promised me when I depended on Him. I was comforted.

Suddenly, an idea popped into my mind. I nodded and smiled as if having a conversation with myself. This could work, giving me some deep insight into their thoughts. I would do it.

Our reunion had been delightful—lots of cooking together and playing games. The December jigsaw puzzle was set out for whomever wanted to work on it. Mark, Benjy, and Deeanne were concentrated on the puzzle, and the groundnut stew simmered on the stove. This was the perfect opportunity for my clandestine interview with our youngest. I invited Heidi to join me on the back porch.

"Heidi, I have a question for you." She plopped down beside me on the steps where we could be alone and pulled our calico cat onto her lap.

"Tell me your favorite thing that happened with your ICA friends." Her eyes lit up as she detailed Bryndon's birthday party and how she got to serve the cake.

"What made you happy?" . . . "What frustrated you?" my line of questioning continued as I hoped to make her feel comfortable as she delved into her eight-year-old memory bank.

And then I popped the question that I thought could reveal deep insight: "So if you could change your life to be any way you want it to be right now, what would you change?"

Her little brow furrowed as she peered up at me and shrugged. "I don't know."

I explained more by giving her some ideas: "Do you wish I homeschooled you? Or do you wish we lived in America instead of Ghana? That sort of thing."

"Oh, I get it now. No, I don't want to be homeschooled, and I don't want to live in America. I would change my life so that we had a swimming pool in our yard and I had my very own tape recorder." Her answers were the most materialistic of our three kids, but she was only eight.

Fourth-grader Deeanne was my middle child who seemed to tip-toe through life with her antennas at high alert. After my initial small talk, I asked her: "Sweetheart, if you could change your life to be any way you wanted it to be right this moment, what would you change?"

Like Heidi, she was perplexed by my question. I gave her the same examples I had given to her younger sister. Homeschooling and a move to America were also not on her wish list.

"Let me think. I would change my life so that Grammy came to live with us all the time," she said.

"That would be super special. I'd love to have my mother here too! Anything else?"

"I would make it so that Marcie's family moved back here to Kumasi because I miss her." Her best missionary-kid friend, whose family ministered here with the Navigators, had recently moved to South Africa.

Deeanne's answers were the most relational of the three.

My oldest, Benjy, was always vocal about how awesome boarding school was. I wasn't worried that he wasn't leveling with me about how he was faring at school. But I still wanted to get his answers to my questions. Sitting on his bed, while we flipped through the pages of his stamp collection, I broached the subject.

"Benjy, I have a question for you—something I've been wondering about."

"Sure, Mom. What is it?"

"If you could change your life to be just how you would like it to be right now, what would you change? Would you like to be homeschooled, or do you wish we lived in America all the time? Or anything else you would like to change if you could?"

This time, I decided to give the examples right away.

"Well, I don't want to be homeschooled, and I don't want to live in America—just visit sometimes like we already do." He then studied the ceiling briefly, deep in thought. I wasn't prepared for what was coming—the most spiritual answer of the three.

"You know, Mom, if I could change my life to be just perfect, I would change myself so that I would be the best Christian I could be, telling people about Jesus all the time, everywhere I go. And you know what, Mom? Maybe someday I'll be like that."

Wow! Why did I worry?

I learned that God is able to work in my children's lives whether they are physically with me or not.

1 Samuel 1:27–28 (NASB): "For [these children] I prayed, and the Lord has given me my petition which I asked of Him. So I have also dedicated [them] to the Lord; as long as [they live they are] dedicated to the Lord." And [she] worshiped the Lord there [additions mine].

# Chapter Twenty-Five

# When Our Kids' Valuables Were Stolen

## July 1988 ~ Lisbon, Portugal

A PERK OF SERVING overseas was visiting other countries while traveling to and from Africa. Since our flight had to land somewhere in Europe, this added minimal cost to the air tickets. At this time, no airlines flew directly between Ghana and the U.S.

On our way home, we planned to visit two sets of missionary friends in Portugal and Spain. Our kids were twelve, ten, and nine years old—perfect ages for experiencing other cultures. Both hosts' families included kids around the same age as ours.

Our hosts in Portugal were John and Linn Crowe. John was Mark's roommate who had warned him about spending so much time with me during our time in college. How special to reunite with the Crowes after more than a decade.

As we began our preparation for travel, I told our kids: "You can choose your favorite things to take to America in your carry-on. You will be responsible for carrying it, but what you want to pack is your choice." They understood the parameters and headed to their bedrooms to make their choices.

I busied myself with a different criteria for my husband's and my carry-ons: not our favorite things, but rather the most needed items for a family traveling for a week in Europe. My items were uninspiring ones such as toiletries, changes of clothes, passports, and vaccination booklets.

"Buckle your seat belts and put your tray tables into their upright positions," the flight attendant spoke on the intercom as we circled Lisbon before landing. Our two daughters wiggled with eagerness, craning their necks to see the ground coming into view. It never ceased to amaze me that we could be quickly transported from our life in Africa to an entirely new-to-us country and culture with simply a ride in a jet.

We passed through customs and spotted our friends waving to us on the other side of the glass door. Anxiety always lessened for me when I could see the ones who were meeting us. The adults hugged, and we introduced our three children to their three as they shyly studied each other.

We threw our carry-ons into the back of the van and clambered into our seats. Our host told us that our first stop would be the zoo before we headed down country to where the Crowes lived. The children squealed with joy, and I heard "oh boy!" from our son.

After two hours of gawking at the animals, we headed back to the van. The chattering of six children filled my ears as our two families walked together. The cool air made me wrap my sweater a bit tighter, and I reached for my youngest daughter's hand. The smell of the animals from the zoo was still clinging to us as we made our way to their vehicle through the shade of the jacaranda trees.

In a manner of seconds our mood shifted from frivolity to devastation as we saw the open door of the van like a gaping wound when the pain suddenly kicks into gear.

We had been robbed.

We climbed into the van and looked for our belongings to determine what was missing. The camera bag: gone. Each of the children's carry-on bags: gone. As we drove to the police station, more and more was discovered to be missing.

Our youngest daughter burst into tears when she realized her Cabbage Patch doll was stolen. Her favorite treasure. The doll she slept with. The doll she clung to when sad. Her little nine-year-old security blanket. Gone.

Our middle child turned white with anxiety and bowed her head. Her Cabbage Patch doll with her shiny black shoes and lacy socks was also gone. The special little tape recorder she had received at Christmas was now in the hands of a thief.

Feeling numb all over, I silently cried out to God. "Oh Father, I accept it when you test me. But do you have to test my children too? They are just baby Christians."

As I comforted my kids over the next few days, I reminded them that "stuff" can be replaced—that possessions are temporary in this world. God, people, and His Word are eternal and those we cannot "lose" from an eternal perspective. We still had each other and our salvation that no one could steal from us. We could put this wound behind us and still enjoy this time in Portugal.

As I watched our three children join hands to jump into the pool—each in varying improvised swimsuits from our hosts, their laughter poured fragrant perfume onto my soul.

God orchestrated growth in my children's lives too, even when I wanted to protect them from any hardship. It is in the struggles of life that we grow—including our children.

My youngest called out to me, interrupting my reflections. "Mommy, jump in. The water is fine!" Life was moving on without dolls and tape recorders. We still had each other.

Even better than that, we possessed the greatest gift of all—our salvation.

And no one can steal that!

John 10:28: I give them eternal life, and they will never perish, and no one will snatch them out of my hand.

# Chapter Twenty-Six

# A Treasure Born in a Village

**February 1993 ~ Tamale, Ghana**

"NINE MONTHS AGO, WE were surprised to find out that Amy was pregnant," Mark wrote in our prayer letter. "Shock quickly changed to excitement, but six weeks later, on June 8, 1992, God called this life back to Himself. All five of us discovered that our family was not yet complete. We prayed, but Amy miscarried two more times. At this time, a village woman fifteen miles away also became pregnant." This is her story as told to us by her brother-in-law.

November 1992 ~ Pong-Tamale, Ghana

The mud hut was dark inside, with a small kerosene lantern glowing on the floor beside the laboring teen. "One more push," her aunt said as other women buzzed around. A tiny infant was thrust into the world and gasped for her first drink of air. Then she cried, which sounded more like a mewing kitten.

"The blood is coming too much," was whispered among the tending ladies. The aunt swaddled the newborn and knelt near Sanatu's face. "Look, child, you have a beautiful baby girl."

Eighteen-year-old Sanatu raised herself on her elbow with the strength she could muster. A tear trickled down her sweaty face as the aunt pressed the infant's cheek against hers.

Sanatu gasped, coughed, and fell back onto her flat pillow. Her eyes and mouth froze in an open position, and her chest stopped its up-and-down movement. The baby gave a feeble cry, with limbs flailing wildly as her mother went completely limp.

The attending ladies began to wail. The atmosphere in the hut changed from the frenzy of labor and birth to the necessity of death's protocols. There was no sound of a new mother cooing to her baby, no taste of colostrum as a newborn suckled, and no movement of a steady heartbeat the baby had felt for the last months in utero. The stench of blood filled the air.

Happiness morphed into sorrow.

For all practical purposes, the baby was forgotten.

⟫⟫ ⟪⟪

The newborn's cries of hunger pierced the night, awakening her grandmother. She grabbed the colorfully painted metal bowl and dipped water from the clay pot. She picked up the crying baby, who began rooting for the breast. "There is nothing there," the grandmother whispered as she offered the infant sips of water from an aluminum spoon.

This went on for some days, waiting for the infant to follow her mother to the grave. The belief at that time was that the baby had caused the mother's death, and if she were allowed to live, she would cause someone else to die.

A friend of the baby's uncle, Ahmedu, arrived on his motorcycle for one of his frequent visits. He heard the story of his friend's sister's death after giving birth. "What happened to the baby then?" he asked.

"She's still alive. We are giving her water because we have no milk. I don't think she will live much longer," the uncle said as he led Ahmedu to see the infant.

Moved with compassion, Ahmedu asked permission to take the child to the hospital. Because the baby's father was only eighteen and her grandfather was deceased, the father's oldest brother "owned" the child and decided her fate. Following the culture tradition, Ahmedu and the baby's uncle asked the chief for permission to take the infant to the hospital. The chief gave his consent.

The ladies who attended her birth wrapped the baby in cloths for the motorcycle ride. Ahmedu straddled his bike, and his friend got on behind him. The tiny baby was handed to her uncle in an attempt to save her life.

Ahmedu propped the motorcycle on its kickstand and led the way to the hospital's main entrance. They passed people in various stages of illnesses or injuries sitting on the steps and in the grass waiting to be seen. When they reached the registration desk and explained the situation, the nurse in her green dress with a white apron said, "I'm sorry. The hospital doesn't accept orphans. You will have to take her to the orphanage."

Back on the motorcycle, they headed to the orphanage on the other side of town where they completed a few formalities, including bringing a bucket and paying the first small monthly fee. The infant also needed a name to be enrolled. In northern Ghana, a person's last name is her father's first name. She was unceremoniously given the name Zenabu for her first name and Alhassan for her last name. Now, she could be enrolled and given some formula.

⟫⟫⟫   ⟪⟪⟪

"Madam Aisha, there is a new baby in the orphanage. She is very tiny," Mohammed said as he leaned on his crutches. His parents had deserted him because he was born disabled. At seventeen years old, he was like a big brother to all the young children. Most orphans returned to their extended families when they turned three years old because that was when they could start working. Boys were especially valued. But disabled Mohammed was never reclaimed. The orphanage had been his home since soon after birth.

A few days later, when I finished buying fruit and vegetables in the market, I stopped by the orphanage to meet the new enrollee. Recently, we had brought an eight-month-old girl to our home for a few days to love on her. The orphanage administrators allowed and encouraged home visits for the orphans because they knew personal attention was good for them. Perhaps I could bring this new baby to our home.

But when I saw the tiny infant, my chest tightened. At three weeks old, she appeared to weigh less than five pounds. Her pint-size body hardly made a bump in her crib. "Would you like to take her for a home visit?" Grace asked me with a sparkle in her eye. She knew I loved the children.

"Not this time," I said. That preemie baby should have been in an incubator or getting oxygen or something. She was probably not going to make it. I would be traumatized if she died while in my care.

My stomach churned as I returned to our narrow, cement-block home. Our house reminded me of a fourteen-foot-wide trailer with a kitchen and living area on one end and a narrow hall with three bedrooms and a bathroom on the other. It was perfect for us.

My seventh grader met me at the door: "Did you bring that baby home for a visit?" Her eyes danced with anticipation of an affirmative answer.

"Well, no—not this time. She looks premature and should probably be in an incubator." I didn't reveal my fear of her possibly dying in our house.

Heidi sank onto the sofa, letting her head fall back on the brown plaid cushion. "Mom!" she moaned, giving *Mom* a couple of extra syllables. "We can handle that. She needs us. Come on."

The entire family gathered, wanting all the details of my visit. My husband sided with the girls, urging me to return and bring the infant for a home visit. Our son was noncommittal. He is a definite "go-with-the-flow" kind of guy.

"Let's ask the Lord for wisdom," my husband said.

I headed back to the orphanage.

Zenabu was a living example of the fragility of life. Her deep charcoal skin stretched thinly over her rib cage. If I looked closely, I could see the throb of a minuscule heart. When I took her back a few days later, I carefully laid her in the crib—the spark of possibility wrapped up in a baby blanket.

Three weeks later, Ginia, a fellow missionary who lived next door to us, wanted to donate some toys to the orphanage. She asked me to accompany her and introduce her to the workers. The brown, one-story building appeared dull and dusty as we walked up with our arms laden with colorful toys. Children stopped their play to watch these curious white ladies mount the steps.

After introductions and giving over the toys, Ginia and I went to visit Zenabu. She was in her crib as if I had just placed her there, though it had been several weeks ago. I bent over the rail, cooing her name: "Hi Zenabu, sweetheart! How are you?"

Her six-week-old eyes became like saucers, and she began to pump her clenched fists in the air and kick her feet as if trying to dog paddle. Ginia lifted the infant to her shoulder and said, "It seems you are happy to have some visitors, little one."

Zenabu's head bobbed from left to right, following my voice to find me. Her searching dark eyes locked with mine and her rosebud lips opened as if she was about to speak. A tsunami of tenderness flooded over me. Ginia said, "Amy, she remembers you!"

I wondered if Zenabu was thinking: "My mommy came back."

⟫⟫⟫ ⟪⟪⟪

Sometimes my heart got all tangled up with my mind, and I wasn't sure what to do. That was how I felt when my husband and daughters repeatedly spoke about adopting Zenabu. We were fresh off the sadness of losing my pregnancies. During family devotions one night, Heidi said, "I don't get it. We want a baby and she needs a family. So why can't we adopt her?"

My mind tried to reason with my heart. We had three teenagers. I'd recently suffered a third miscarriage. I was almost forty.

I grappled in the blackness of night with questions: How would she feel growing up in a white family? What would Ghanaians say when we took one of them and made her one of us? What would our supporters say since we had to raise support per family member? We couldn't just say we would tighten our belts and have another child. What would it be like for her when we returned to America and she was a minority instead of majority?

A month later, my husband walked through the market stalls, shaking hands and conversing with his Muslim friends. He saw a young Caucasian couple at another merchant's table and began talking with them. Kevin and Nora were from Ireland and had come to Ghana to visit his childhood home north of Tamale. Mark said, "Would you like to join my wife and me for lunch? We live on the outskirts of town." They said yes and followed him to our home.

Kevin rested his arm on the back of Nora's chair. "I grew up here in Ghana. I have brought my new wife to visit and learn about my childhood setting. My parents were in Bible translation."

As we chatted, I told them about the orphan we had kept in our home for three days. I remembered the feel of Zenabu's tiny hand hanging onto my finger as if staking a claim to it and refusing to let go. I tried to shake off the emotional memory.

"What a coincidence!" Kevin said. "The same thing happened to my family when I was eight. Someone brought us a baby girl whose mother had died in childbirth, and we took her in to save her life. We fell in love with her and ended up adopting her. She is my eighteen-year-old sister."

My mouth opened, but no sound came out. My chest began to tingle. Had I heard him correctly? Had this stranger my husband happened upon experienced the life decision that was before us—to adopt an orphaned baby whose mother had died in childbirth? Once I could straighten out my running-rampant thoughts, I asked Kevin my four questions.

"How does your sister feel about growing up in a white family?"

Kevin leaned forward. "My mom told me recently that she took her out to eat, and my sister specifically thanked her again for adopting her. Despite our different skin color, she feels blessed to be in our family."

My next question was, "How did Ghanaians react when you adopted her into your family?"

"Ghanaians loved what our adoption showed them. It was a life lesson about how our color and heritage don't matter. We are all a part of the human race. It was a great example of how God adopts us into His family. Also, inheritance is important in Ghanaian culture, and they believe that blood relations rank the highest in inheritance. They were amazed that my sister would inherit from my parents equally to us two biological sons."

"What did your supporters say when you needed more support to adopt her?"

Kevin laughed. "Our supporters were on board and wanted photos of her in every letter. When we went on furlough, she always got the lion's share of attention during our visits to churches."

I asked my final question: "What was it like for her when your family left Ghana to reside in Ireland?"

"She is more Irish than I am! You should hear her accent. The change of location did not affect our closeness as a family. Now that she is of age and can choose where she lives and goes to college, she has chosen Ireland." Kevin crossed his arms and leaned back in his chair as if he had finished a deposition.

Indeed, he had.

I remembered my devotions from the day before in Deuteronomy 30. The Lord spoke to Israel and told them what He commanded them was not too difficult or out of reach. He said that the word was very near them, in their mouths and hearts, that they may observe it.

He went on to say, "See, I have set before you today life and . . . death . . . So choose life in order that you may live, you and your descendants" (NASB). God was referring to choosing life to follow Him in obedience—not turning to idols.

God's words to Israel pierced my heart as if He were reminding me, too: "You know what to do—it is already in your heart."

I thought of that tiny six-week-old jerking her head toward my voice a month earlier in the orphanage.

I thought of my seventh-grade daughter sighing, "I don't understand. We want a baby, and she needs a family. So why can't we adopt her?"

I thought of how God had connected Mark to Kevin and Nora in the market during their brief time in Tamale and then invited them to lunch spur-of-the-moment.

I thought of how my heart burned when Kevin mentioned that orphaned baby being brought to their home.

And I knew God's answer.

After seeing Kevin and Nora off, we retired to our bedroom for our midday siesta. Lying beside my husband, I gently touched his arm. "Mark?"

"Yes?" he said sleepily.

"I think Zenabu might be our daughter."

He bolted to a sitting position. "Really?" He had wanted to adopt her from that first visit, but I had held us back with my philosophical questions. "This morning, I was thinking of the parable in Matthew 13 of the man who found a treasure in a field. He sold all he had to buy the field to get that treasure. I feel like Zenabu is that treasure." After discussing a few more issues, we knelt and asked for wisdom from the One who had given Zenabu life.

The next day, we brought Zenabu to our home as we began the steps to pursue adoption. Even though the proceedings took four months, she had no idea that she wasn't our legal daughter yet. All Zenabu knew was that she was loved and cherished in our home from that day forward.

On June 6, 1993, in the High Court of Tamale, the presiding judge declared that Zenabu Alhassan had a new name: Kinza Zenabu Hagerup. The judge also stated that this child had new parents, Mark and Amy Hagerup—"just as if she had been born to them in lawful marriage."

One year earlier, I was crying with a broken heart when God had called our expected little one home to Him. On this day, I cried with a joyful heart as I embraced our new daughter in the courtroom. God used our surprise pregnancy the previous year to prepare us for desiring more children because He had a special treasure that He planned to add to our family.

We later discovered that in Arabic, "Kinza" means "treasure."

James 1:5: If any of you lacks wisdom, let him ask God, who gives generously to all without reproach, and it will be given him.

# Jeered by the Spectators

**March 1993 ~ Bouaké, Côte d'Ivoire**

EVER SINCE BEN WAS little, he ran with his dad. Once he reached middle school, Ben enjoyed a brisk cup of coffee before dawn and then trekked out with his dad to the university's stadium, located two miles from our Kumasi home. Ben would peel off his shoes and socks and run a mile barefoot while his dad ran three miles.

I loved hearing about our kids' experiences at boarding school. Sometimes I learned about them through their letters, and occasionally I listened to their accounts soon after they occurred.

The following story is about what happened to Ben during his junior year of high school. I didn't find out about this until I read it from an assignment Ben wrote at Penn State for one of his courses.

Here is Ben's account of what transpired:

During my junior year at Ivory Coast Academy, my PE teacher announced the formation of a team for track and field, which would compete with other African schools. Quite a few guys joined for the short sprints and different field events, but no one volunteered to compete in the long-distance runs.

The majority of the students at my boarding school came from families of American missionaries. We knew we didn't stand a chance against our African counterparts. Most of these guys walked miles to school and worked long hours on the family farms afterward. When not in school or working, they would pour themselves into playing soccer. The pressure cooker of the average African boy's life demanded endurance for mere survival. And they were fast!

Despite this, I signed up to run the 3.5-kilometer race and started training.

Three weeks later, the track and field team arrived at the stadium in the middle of the afternoon. A sizeable crowd had gathered in the stands, and the groups of athletes stood haphazardly on the field. The butterflies in my stomach were going crazy. Several team members competed in their respective events, which only heightened my uneasiness.

I thought, *Those Africans run without running. They neither breathe hard nor slow down. And I will be running against them. What was I thinking?*

Finally, the participants in my race were called to the track. I was the only white competing against thirty-nine African guys. Their supple, powerful brown legs and arms mirrored hard work and training. I wondered what would become of me in this unequal race.

The gunshot broke into my restless thoughts. Forty pairs of legs started running: one pair white, the rest black. After the initial fast start from giddiness, I forced myself into a more realistic pace and focused on my breathing. My African opponents, however, never slowed down. That initial fast start became their normal pace. I could not believe it!

Everyone else passed me in less than half a minute, leaving me the caboose of the race. The crowds in the stands stood up and booed at me. "Look at that white boy trying to run . . . He doesn't stand a chance . . . Hey you, give up." A defiant resolution enabled me to shrug off the crowd's discouraging taunts and keep going.

Midway through the run, the first signs of fatigue—aching and heavy breathing—hammered my body. Though the sun was setting, heat simmered from the track. Inhaling the dry, dusty air left my throat slightly sore. As if this were not enough, the lead runner had just "lapped" me. I wanted to dig a hole in the middle of the track and drop out of sight.

But I was determined to keep going. I maintained my pace and started gaining on two runners. When I passed them, they dived into the unorganized group of athletes watching on the field and tore off the number identifying them, giving up in shame. After passing a few more, my goal rose from just completing the race to not coming in last. At least I could finish with some honor.

The crowd's laughing had quieted down to a dull roar. I continued running and consciously reserved some energy for the home stretch.

One lap from the end, I quickened my pace. Adrenaline and an iron will kept me going even as more fatigue enveloped me. I noticed a runner ten yards ahead of me. "Could I possibly beat him?" I determined to try with all my might.

Before engaging the "afterburners," I steadily approached him from behind. I matched each of his strides with one and a half of my own and slowly reeled him in. I could hear his heavy breathing, smell his sweat, and feel his aching legs.

The time had come: I switched lanes and opened up the throttle. With my heart racing and legs pumping furiously, I edged past him.

To my surprise, the crowd stood up and began cheering for me. The roar of applause shocked me into yet a faster pace. Without looking back, I sprinted fiercely to the finish line.

I had completed the race and endured until the end, winning a tremendous personal victory.

Realizing the anguish my son endured was tough for me. But it was evident Ben had persisted, and God had used this trial to grow him in maturity. I was in awe of the wonder of God at work in my son. The only part I had in Ben's trial was through prayer for him—not prayer for the race—but prayer for spiritual growth and strength when facing trials.

Sometimes, God uses me in my children's lives to encourage them to grow spiritually. And sometimes, He uses other people or circumstances to work in their lives by the power of His Spirit in them.

I am not the determining factor in whom God uses in my children's lives. That is God's privilege.

But I have been entrusted with the best weapon for influencing them: prayer.

Colossians 4:12: A servant of Christ Jesus . . . always struggling on your behalf in his prayers, that you may stand mature and fully assured in all the will of God.

# Chapter Twenty-Eight

# A Grandfather's Act of Mercy

**February 1995 ~ Arlington Heights, IL**

THE PHONE'S JINGLE INTERRUPTED my morning Bible reading. Our two high school daughters had left for the bus, and twenty-one-month-old Kinza played at my feet. "We have six African American babies due to be born in the next few weeks and no home to place them. Your friend gave us your name as someone who might be interested. Are you open to adopting again?" the lady from the Chicago Child Services paused as she waited for my reply.

"Let me talk to my husband and get back to you," I said as I handed our toddler some wooden blocks.

Our pastor's wife came over later that morning to share and pray together. I told her about the desperate call still echoing in my mind. Mark and I had been grappling with whether to adopt another child even before this request from Child Services came.

Donna glanced over at my toddler stacking blocks in the corner. "There is so much for our children to learn in the workshop of the family. You are already committed to the growing up years again. Adopting another child will not make much difference to you regarding time commitment, but it will make a huge difference for Kinza."

When Mark arrived home, I shared the request with him. We knelt and asked the God of the universe for His clear direction for us and our family.

We felt sorry for those babies about to be born with no placement in sight. But we didn't have peace about pursuing a stateside adoption, which could delay our return to Ghana. Also, if we were to adopt again, we wanted our children to share the heritage of being Ghanaians.

As we were leaving our bedroom, Mark said: "If God has another child for us, He will have to make it clear by providing the support we would need to raise." I didn't think that was likely to happen.

Mom's Day Out was a church-sponsored program where mothers dropped off their little ones so they could run errands child-free. I enjoyed working in this program every Wednesday to earn extra cash.

Debbie handed a toddler to me as she welcomed another mom and baby. The nursery was bustling with workers preparing the room, moms dropping off, and toddlers and preschoolers grabbing their favorite toys. Things settled down once all the children were there. We sat them at the low table for snack time.

As Debbie poured the goldfish crackers onto each napkin, she addressed me: "Amy, Larry and I were talking last night, and we want you and Mark to know that if you want to adopt again, we will support the baby. We will also network with our friends to raise the rest of the support you need."

She continued nonchalantly pouring crackers, not realizing she had just dropped a bombshell on me. I felt like I had read a positive pregnancy test. My thoughts tumbled like rolled dice in my brain: Was my baby just born? Was my baby just conceived? Where is my baby? How soon can I be united with him or her?

I was eager to tell Mark that God had another child for us!

December 1995 ~ Tamale, Ghana

I leaned forward on our brown plaid sofa cushions, trying to be sure I'd caught every word that Gaboy shared about the birth of his grandchild. Twenty-two months earlier, in February 1994, a baby girl had been born in Salvego. Her paternal grandfather, who sat before us now, had saved her life. Here is what he shared with us that night. (I have changed his story from first person to third person for clarity.)

Gaboy sat outside the mud hut, awaiting an update on his sick daughter-in-law, who had given birth one week earlier. The young mother was only twelve or thirteen, and the baby's father, Gaboy's son, was sixteen. Suddenly what the grandfather dreaded most happened—the wailing began inside the hut. The child's mother was gone.

A few days later, Gaboy realized that the village ladies were unwilling to wet-nurse the newborn. The relatives gave the infant water in sips from a spoon whenever she cried. But, of course, the baby needed milk to survive.

Gaboy jumped on his black "made-in-Taiwan" bicycle, pedaling as if his fury would result in a bottle of milk. When he reached the nearest town, he searched out the social worker. Modesto listened with interest to Gaboy's plea to save Ishetu, an orphaned newborn.

Modesto pulled on his helmet and handed Gaboy a spare one. Dirt flew up behind the wheels as they retraced the path to Salvego.

They entered the dark hut, and Gaboy picked up the infant. Her eyes were sunken; the cloth under her bottom was dry.

After lifting the tiny baby girl into his arms, Modesto asked the gathered relatives to take him to a breastfeeding mother. They led him to a nearby courtyard filled with young ladies. Sadly, they shook their heads no. There were plenty of breastfeeding women in the village, but none were willing to take the risk of nursing a baby whose mother had died. They believed that if they did so, they could suffer the same fate.

Modesto handed the child to Gaboy as they returned to where his motorcycle was parked. Now, a party of three mounted the Yamaha: thirtyish Modesto, fortyish Gaboy, and one-week-old Ishetu. The starving infant was showing signs of dehydration and would not survive much longer. Time was of the essence.

At the next village, the quest was made again—to find a woman willing to wet-nurse Ishetu so she would survive the trip to the orphanage. Again, the answer was no. Modesto didn't give up.

A small group of curious onlookers surrounded the motorcycle's riders in the third village. Modesto explained the plight of the starving baby. One young mom with her baby on her hip listened intently as she heard the story.

Perhaps the young mother touched the baby's fingers or locked eyes with the infant. I don't know. But the inborn power of a hungry infant pulling on the inborn compassion of a nursing mother was drawn together like a magnetic force. The young mother handed her baby to a nearby teenager, saying to Modesto, "I will nurse her."

Ishetu survived the trip to the orphanage.

Three months before Gaboy's story captivated us, we had returned from our furlough and were getting unpacked in our Tamale home. When returning from a long absence, we visited and greeted our friends, as was Ghanaian custom. Mark got back into the saddle of preaching at different village churches; we were encouraged that churches were growing.

As our lives normalized after our year's furlough, I thought about finding the final little Hagerup God had for us. Kinza had turned three in November, and we wanted our next child to be close in age to her. Deeanne and Heidi arrived home from boarding school for five weeks in late November. They were also excited about adopting another sibling. Ben was in his sophomore year at Penn State, so he was not with us.

When we were settled enough, I made the investigative trip to the orphanage. Our mission board had preapproved the adoption, and some of the support had already been pledged. The next step was to find our child. We were interested in adopting a boy, primarily because I didn't want to have to braid two heads of hair for the next seventeen years. But I also thought that two girls growing up together would be ideal since they could share clothes, toys, a bedroom, and their feminine interests as they grew up together.

When I got to the orphanage, I greeted all the workers, who were now my friends. I inquired about adoptable boys, but there were none. A malnourished little Fulani girl toddled toward me and reached up to be held. This was unusual because the orphans were initially afraid of a white person, but she seemed fearless and confident, despite her small size.

I picked her up, talked to her, and stroked her head. When I was trying to put her back down, she scissored her legs to my waist to continue to be held. I pried her loose while speaking gently, hoping she wouldn't feel rejected. I thought perhaps this was a sign that she was the child for us. I later found out that she did that to everybody.

When I got home, I told Mark and our high school daughters: "There is no boy available to adopt, but there is a twenty-two-month-old Fulani girl."

"Why don't you bring her for a visit? Go back and get her." That was the consensus. So I went back to the orphanage.

I carried Ishetu from the car, and she clung to me as she entered this strange new world. She sucked her left thumb while glancing around the living room. Three-year-old Kinza tugged on her foot. Two adult-sized girls crooned soft words to her, and one of them took her from me.

Ishetu's arms were like sticks, and her belly was distended, probably from worms. At twenty-two months, she weighed only fourteen pounds. Mark referred to her sparse hair as scrub grass in the desert. When we fed her, she opened her mouth wide as if the size available would be comparable to the input of the food. This child was hungry—both for nourishment and love.

After a few days, we believed she was the child God had for our family. We took her back to the orphanage to find out the name of her birth father and village so we could inquire if she was adoptable.

Ishetu was confused when I took her back. She again squeezed her skinny legs around my middle to prevent me from putting her down. I told her I would be back, but she didn't understand English. Her tears became more desperate as the nanny extricated her from my body. I was also choked up, sensing my child's confusion and grief at me leaving her.

We located her village and talked to her elderly family members. We explained our desire to adopt Ishetu and invited the two grandfathers to visit us after making their decision. They came a few days later and accompanied us to the orphanage to give their approval to the matron. Our Ghanaian liaison, Abdullai, was there to represent us, which was helpful when languages we didn't understand were used. It is common for Africans to speak four or five languages fluently. Abdullai had helped us adopt Kinza three years earlier.

Ishetu saw us from a distance when we got out of our pickup truck and came toddling down the path. I picked her up, shifting the diaper bag to my other shoulder. I had brought clothes for her so we could leave the orphanage-provided garments there.

Seated in the hot office with the grandfathers, we explained to the matron, who had her arms tightly crossed, our desire to adopt Ishetu. Her jaw was taut as she addressed the grandfathers in their dialect: "Don't you know these people are trying to steal your child away from you?"

Abdullai knew that dialect, so he said: "Oh, madam. That is not true. Tell them the truth."

The matron switched to another language: "Give her to someone else. They already have one child they have adopted." But Abdullai knew that language too, so he again came to our defense.

Pulling down her glasses and peering over their rims, she glared at Abdullai and slammed shut the file. "It is close to Christmas now; we will close for the holidays. Come back in January, and we can discuss this more then." With that declaration, she briskly left the room with her heels clicking as she marched across the porch.

I felt frozen in place—the fate of Ishetu, still snuggled up on my lap, barked out as if she were a book I wanted to check out. My husband took my arm to force me to stand.

Abdullai lifted the little one from me and carried her partway down the dirt path toward the nanny coming to retrieve her. Ishetu's cries entered my heart and squeezed it like a rope capturing a calf.

We returned to our house, where Mark dropped me off before taking the grandfathers to their village. As I got out of the back seat, Gaboy said, "Don't worry, Madam. You will soon have your baby."

Deeanne and Heidi figured out what happened without asking for details: Mom had come home with red eyes and no baby. They watched as I put away the crib and high chair I had set up for Ishetu. The only thing still in hopeful anticipation was the diaper bag, which I left packed up just in case. I placed it in the bottom of the closet, wincing as I closed the door.

⟫⟫⟫ ⟪⟪⟪

About a week later, we were hosting a Christmas dinner for some of our Ghanaian friends. I was cooking two large pots of food: groundnut stew and rice. Everything was ready for our guests' arrival in another hour when we heard a knock at the door.

Gaboy and another man were standing on our front porch. The grandfather had brought the social worker to meet us. Modesto peppered us with questions, including details about our adoption of Kinza.

After about thirty minutes of interrogation, Modesto stated that he had decided we should have Ishetu. This was perplexing because we were under the impression that the matron at the orphanage had the authority over who received this baby. "I have more power than she does because I am the one who enrolled the child. Because of that, I can also remove her from the orphanage," Modesto said.

I felt my insides flutter at this news, and I grabbed Mark's arm. "When can we get her?"

"Right now!" Modesto said with a broad grin.

Putting Deeanne and Heidi in charge of receiving our dinner guests, I grabbed the still-packed diaper bag out of the closet. We headed outside with Modesto and Gaboy right behind us.

My heart pounded double-time as Mark drove to the orphanage. I strained through the inky night to see if the matron's light was on in her home. It was. "You stay here," Modesto said as he slammed the truck's door and joined Gaboy, mounting the front steps of her house.

The wait seemed to take forever. Mark and I sat in silence, lost in thought about the gravity of what was happening inside those closed doors—a power struggle over the destiny of a tiny orphan's life. Who would win?

Finally, someone pulled open my back door, and two little brown arms extended toward me.

I reached out to receive Ishetu and snuggled her close to my chest. Her tiny arms wrapped around my neck as we sat there, cheek to cheek.

God had won.

Psalm 9:10: And those who know your name put their trust in you, for you, O Lord, have not forsaken those who seek you.

# Chapter Twenty-Nine

# Adoption: Blocked

**Early 1996 ~ Tamale, Ghana**

I PLACED ISHETU IN her crib and stroked her wiry hair. I repeated my nightly message to her before I prayed: "Daddy loves you. Mommy loves you. Your siblings love you. And Jesus loves you most of all." Her arms stayed outstretched toward me, begging me to pick her up again for one more cuddle. The soothing words I whispered helped her feel safe and she settled for the night.

I wondered what she was thinking. Did she remember when I held her close and then returned her to the orphanage? Did she recall clinging to me while another wrenched her from my arms? Did she harbor the trauma of not having the words to call out, "Don't leave me!" when she saw me walk away?

She sucked vigorously on her thumb, and her body relaxed into the sheet with tiny yellow ducks printed on it. Slowly, her eyes closed and she succumbed to sleep. I stroked her head, asking God to give her to us if that was His perfect plan.

We began all the formalities to adopt Ishetu, which included ob-taining a birth certificate. Gaboy was instrumental in this process, making multiple trips to the Registry for Births office. When he was being interviewed, the official pressed him for his original national-ity. Gaboy, the paternal grandfather, and the maternal grandfather had arrived as three-year-olds with their parents from Burkina Faso. They had grown up in Ghana, married, and had children. Ishetu was the first of their grandchildren to live in the same Fulani settlement, where they watched cattle.

With the news of Gaboy's original country, the official put on Ishetu's birth certificate that she was a citizen of Burkina Faso. Nei-ther she nor her parents had ever lived there.

When our lawyer studied the birth certificate, he shook his head in disgust. "Why did he do this?" he said as he started to pace. Shaking the certificate at us, he continued, "No Ghanaian judge is going to give you a Burkinabe child." He paused as if to let that sink into our brains. "I am dropping your case."

My husband and I were silent on the bumpy ride home—the fresh wounds from his resignation still bleeding inside us. We knew our town had no pool of lawyers from whom to choose. Hiring another lawyer would mean multiple trips to Accra, an eleven-hour drive one way. I went through the motions to prepare supper for the four of us. Our high school daughters were at boarding school so were unaware of this turn of events.

After reading bedtime stories to the little girls, I picked up Ishetu to put her into her crib. I knelt beside her bed each night to pray with her. Feeling defeated, I could hardly get the words out. "Dear Jesus," I stammered. Then I heard this sweet little toddler say, "'ear 'esus." I realized Ishetu must have thought I was telling her to pray by repeating after me, which I sometimes did. So, I adapted the prayer of my bruised heart to come from her innocent perspective instead.

With the appropriate pauses, Ishetu prayed after me: "Please give me to this family . . . I need a family . . . And I want to learn about You . . . You can do anything . . . I love You . . . In Jesus' name, amen."

Tears were spilling out of my eyes now. I crept outside in the darkness, pulling one of our string lawn chairs under the mango tree. The muscular branches weighed down with green mangoes mirrored the load hanging from my heart. I continued my dialogue with the heavenly Burden-lifter.

"Father in heaven, the Red Sea is in front of us. This is a humanly impossible situation. The lawyer won't take the case. Only You can part the Red Sea. All we can do is stand by and see your salvation just like the children of Israel did when they faced the Red Sea. I don't know what You will do, but I know You can solve this problem somehow."

Just then, it began to rain. I felt like the Lord was crying with me. It was the first shower of the rainy season, making it even more significant. The Lord brought to my mind Hosea 6:3: "Let us know, let us press on to know the Lord. His going forth is as certain as the dawn; And He will come to us like the rain, Like the spring rain watering the earth" (NASB).

I knew the Lord would answer me—just like He sent the rain and just like the sun would rise tomorrow. I only had to wait on Him. And trust Him.

A few days later, our lawyer sent a message to come to his office. When we arrived, he said, "I've decided to take your adoption case. I know what I'm going to do."

We didn't know what had changed his mind, but we did know Who had changed it.

On April 17, 1996, Ishetu Alhassan became Colette Ishetu Hagerup—just like God had planned for her since the beginning of time.

No human can thwart what God's will is for a person.

Exodus 14:13–14: And Moses said to the people, "Fear not, stand firm, and see the salvation of the Lord, which he will work for you today. For the Egyptians whom you see today, you shall never see again. The Lord will fight for you, and you have only to be silent."

# God's Purpose Seen in Life and Death

# Chapter Thirty

# Runaway Dad is Located

**May 1970 (age 16) ~ Columbia, SC**

FROM THE DAY MY father deserted our family, he never sent any child support. Despite Mama's financial struggles, she prioritized providing us kids with high-quality shoes. I'm not sure what her thinking entailed, but perhaps she believed proper-fitting, quality shoes were required for healthy feet. Whenever I was blessed with a new pair of shoes during my teen years, I noticed my old pair disappeared from my closet. The next day before we left for school, I would see my old pair on Mama's feet.

We prayed regularly for my father to be saved and to return to us. Finally, God gave us a glimpse of our dad in an unexpected manner. When I was a junior in high school, Anna, who had type one diabetes, went into a diabetic coma. She was seriously ill, and somehow, my father found out about it. He traveled to South Carolina to see her.

Anna was at the Baptist Hospital, located downtown right beside Columbia High School, where I attended. Once school was out, I was to meet my dad at the hospital. When I told my English lit. teacher, Mr. Webb, what was happening, he allowed me to leave class before the final bell rang. Most of my teachers knew about our family situation because my dad had attended this same high school twenty-five years earlier. Miss Purvis, my home room and biology teacher, had taught my father too. When she asked me if I was related to George Roth, I told her he was my father. A bright look flashed across her face but quickly disappeared when I told her he had deserted our family when I was ten. With compassion in her usually stern voice, she said, "Well, he's the loser."

From that moment on, she treated me with favor.

I entered the hospital's main door and glanced nervously around the lobby. A profound awkwardness seeped through my veins as I caught sight of the man who happened to be my biological father. His bald head and handlebar mustache made him appear different than I remembered and yet eerily the same. Our first interaction is a blur, but I'm sure it was polite with "yes, sir" and "no, sir" that I had been taught.

Our focus was on my recovering sister, who was out of a coma now. Anna and I had grown close during our teenage years. Since she had moved in with our grandparents several years earlier, we didn't have much time together. Even with that separation, we still maintained the camaraderie of being sisters. Not having a father in our home did not rob us of supportive family relationships.

Anna was propped up in her elevated bed with her mousey blonde hair spread out on the white pillowcase. She sipped Sprite from a giant cup and then set it down on her tray beside an open

*Seventeen* magazine. Her shoes were positioned neatly under her bed, waiting to be put into action: Anna would be discharged soon. I rushed to her side and threw my arms around her neck, almost knocking over her drink. I wonder if Dad felt the affection between his two oldest daughters, whom he hadn't seen for years. If so, did his heart yearn to be a recipient of that love too?

It was Dad's turn next. Anna interacted with our dad much differently than I did. She wasn't intimidated and confronted him with a snide comment: "Well, look who's here. It's about time!" Then she laughed and hugged him when he got close to her. I parked myself on a metal chair in her room and tried to make myself invisible while they talked about nothing of consequence.

Later, when my dad drove me home, he asked me questions about my life outside school. "I spend many evenings babysitting, but I can't be out late on school nights. Rocky often waits for me to get home from a job so we can talk. We are very close."

"That's good. Have you saved any money?" he asked, and I told him I had.

"How much have you saved?"

"Just over $500 now. I'm saving for college," I said.

"That's great. Hey, I need some cash right now. Would you be willing to give me that $500?" he asked. "If you give it to me, I can get you a compact foreign car my friend is selling. Would you like to have your own car?"

I was usually compliant when asked for help—my mother often needed me to buy milk or bread. But perhaps because of my dad's history with me (or lack thereof), I politely refused his request. I gazed out the car window, hoping to change the direction of our conversation. "That is where I went to junior high," I said as we passed Wardlaw. I didn't possess much assertiveness, and he made me nervous. Thankfully, he dropped the money issue.

When Dad was leaving the next day, he promised to keep in touch with us. As I stood beside his rental car, saying goodbye, he gave me his phone number and address. I glanced at the paper in my hands and felt a flicker of hope this might be a turning point—that my father would be in my life again.

But the phone call to the number a few days later resulted in the monotone recording: "This number is no longer in service." And my letter came back stamped: "Addressee moved. No forwarding address." The flicker of hope evaporated into nothingness.

The returned letter indicated I had been deserted all over again. But I wasn't devastated; it felt more like a fact than an emotion. I gave ten-year-old Polly, writing at the table, a kiss on her cheek as I stroked her blonde hair. I stuck my head into Rocky's room to see what he was doing. My brother was super intelligent and always worked on radios or complex math problems. He showed me the cassette tape he was repairing. I kicked off my comfy shoes in my bedroom and flopped on my black-and-white houndstooth bedspread. I love my family.

❈

Seven years later

I had graduated from Columbia Bible College, gotten married in Ethiopia, had our first child, and was now on furlough in my hometown, Columbia. At the same time, Mark was attending Columbia Graduate School, working toward his master's degree in missions. I was pregnant with our second child.

Being reunited with my family always filled me with warmth and contentment. During our first term in Ethiopia, I missed two family weddings. Anna and her husband, Kerry, married soon after Benjy was born in 1976. Rocky and Linda married in June 1977. Kerry, his young son, Jeremy, and Linda were delightful additions to our family. My youngest sibling, Polly, was a freshman at Columbia Bible College, still living at home.

The significant need currently was for funds to pay for Polly's college. Mama spent time on her knees, praying for God's provision. One day, she thought of using social security for financial assistance.

She was aware of some of the laws and realized that if our father had died without our knowledge, she could collect support for Polly to help pay the college bills. Mama contacted the social security office, provided my dad's social security number, and inquired about the possibility of declaring him deceased if he had not been paying social security.

An envelope from the Social Security Administration arrived in her mailbox. The news was that George Roth had been found—his New Jersey address was included. Mama was stunned at this news and told my older sister about the letter, saying, "I don't know what to do."

Anna quickly responded, "Give the address to me. I will write him." She wrote a short letter to him, saying that she was his oldest daughter (married with a new last name) and he should call her if he wanted more information. And that was it.

The letter didn't get returned this time.

⇶⇶⇶ ⇇⇇⇇

Anna sat on the floor playing with our toddler son who was sporting adorable shoes. I embraced Mama's philosophy of the importance of high-quality shoes. That the shoes were cute was a side benefit. Anna was giving my husband and me a date night out. "Look at this, Benjy," she crooned as she made the stuffed bear dance on the end table. Anna's antics were interrupted by the shrill ring of the phone. "Just a minute, sweetie," she called out to Benjy as he continued to play. Anna grabbed the receiver just as the third ring began. "Hello?"

Her eyes widened as she took in the first words that she heard: "Anna, this is your father."

⇶⇶⇶ ⇇⇇⇇

Anna told us later that when she realized who was calling, she had to reach out to the paneled wall to steady herself. Dad continued, "I got your letter and decided to call. How are you?" Anna filled him in on her marriage and stepson. Meanwhile, Benjy was curious, so he grabbed the stuffed bear and toddled over to where she stood.

"Hang on. I want you to speak to someone." Anna then held the phone to Benjy and told him to say hi. Benjy babbled some baby talk, unable to comprehend the significance of hearing this man's voice, who happened to be his maternal grandfather.

When Anna took the receiver back, my dad said, "Is that your child?"

"No. He's Amy's."

My dad arranged to fly south to see all four of us kids in January 1978. He planned to take each of us out to eat for private conversations. I had recently given birth to our second child, Deeanne, on her aunt Polly's eighteenth birthday. So tiny Deeanne accompanied me on this estranged father/abandoned daughter meeting. Having my infant there brought an incongruous tenderness to the tough occasion.

During my dinner with him, my dad told me I could ask him whatever I wanted. My mother taught us to love and pray for him rather than judge him. As I thought about this prompting, I couldn't think of any question to ask him. He got the ball rolling: "If you were to ask me why I left your mother and you kids, I would say that I was temporarily insane."

That loosened my tongue. "Then why didn't you come back when your sanity returned?"

He responded that he owed my grandparents money and didn't want to return until he had enough to repay them. He also said that he had started to come back several times but would get scared and go back. I didn't believe that because of other lies he had told me, like his contact information that was fake. But that didn't matter now.

What mattered was that he was making the effort. He was interested in becoming a part of our close-knit family (minus our mother).

Again, I was given an address and a phone number so we could keep in contact.

This time, it worked—we were connected and began to build a relationship from the brokenness of our past. I met his live-in girlfriend, Ginny, who later became his wife.

Our mission headquarters at this time was in New Jersey. We were required to stop at SIM's home office at the beginning of each furlough for medicals and debriefing. Because of this, Dad and Ginny were the first family members we visited when we arrived home from Ghana.

Our biggest concern was for their salvation, so Mark and I would witness to them whenever we were together. Ginny was open to discussing the gospel, but my dad constantly changed the subject. We never saw spiritual fruit.

I remember the first time we stayed with Dad and Ginny on our arrival to the U.S. after four years in Ghana. They took us to a local mall with its bright lights and fancy decorated windows. My dad bought our three children (ages six, four, and three) expensive Buster Brown shoes.

Our children walked abreast with my dad and Ginny, holding hands while making satisfying clicking noises with their brand-new shoes. I was walking behind them with Mark.

I felt a prick of bitterness fighting to negate the kindness of his gifts. Those were shoes he should have put on *my* feet.

But then I realized that he was grasping at ways to show love to his descendants and be a part of a close-knit family as best he could.

By buying them quality shoes.

Colossians 3:12–13: Put on then, as God's chosen ones, holy and beloved, compassionate hearts, kindness, humility, meekness, and patience, bearing with one another and, if one has a complaint against another, forgiving each other; as the Lord has forgiven you, so you also must forgive.

# Chapter Thirty-One

# Bad Advice Disguised as Caution

**Spring 1988 ~ Kumasi, Ghana**

OUR MISSIONARY COLLEAGUE LEANED back in his chair, holding his Risk cards like a fan. He crossed one leg over the other as he recounted his recent trip to Tamale. "I am always glad when I leave Tamale: It's powerfully hot. The water supply is sketchy. Electricity comes and goes. Honestly, it seems to be the armpit of Ghana." He ended his rant with a flourish, laying his winning cards on the table, and said, "Pray that you are never assigned to Tamale."

The following year, we were home on furlough. Mark was almost to the finish line of completing his master's in missions at Columbia International University. Prayer days were a monthly occurrence at CIU, but Mark wished they were held more often. These special days were dedicated to prayer and included an esteemed chapel speaker and the cancellation of regular classes.

"Are you willing to do anything for the Lord? Go anywhere the Lord calls you? Anywhere?" The chapel speaker was wrapping up his message. Ushers filled the aisles, sending stacks of small commitment cards down each row. "Take this card, pray over it, and sign it with your response." The three options were praying for missions, giving to missions, and going wherever the Lord would lead.

Mark studied the commitment card during his personal prayer time. "Lord, you know we are doing all three of these things. But I want to renew my commitment to go anywhere for You. Amy and I are willing to move if that is Your plan."

He checked off the three options, signed the card, and stuck it in the back of his Bible.

When he arrived home an hour later, a letter from our Ghana director, where we were serving as missionaries, was in the mailbox. "That's interesting. Why would Ira be sending us a letter?" Mark said. He plopped onto the flowered sofa that came with our furnished rented house.

With me watching over his shoulder, Mark opened the envelope. We silently read the preliminary information about some missionaries retiring. Then our director made his request: "Would you be willing to move to Tamale when you return to Ghana next year?"

Our eyes met after we finished reading. Tamale? The armpit of Ghana? Us?

Mark said, "Amy, you won't believe this, but I just signed a commitment card after chapel today that we would be willing to move anywhere God wants us to go." We had been ministering in Kumasi for eleven years. To move north to Tamale would be a life-changing challenge.

I remembered our fellow missionary the previous year at our kitchen table, lamenting all the hardships of life in Tamale. His words reverberated: "Pray that you are never assigned to Tamale." That reminded me of our first term in Ethiopia when another well-meaning missionary had told me to pray that we wouldn't be assigned to Waka. She had chronicled the hardship of loneliness there. But moving to Waka was God's good plan for us.

Sometimes, well-meaning friends will influence us with a viewpoint that is not from God's perspective. This is essentially bad advice disguised as caution. I have learned to set aside such words of "death" and to instead charge full force into God's revealed direction.

We said yes.

We returned to Ghana in June 1990 and moved to Tamale several months later. Mark and I met Johnson and Lydia—our next-door neighbors and co-laborers in the gospel. Johnson, a fairly new believer, had a mega vision for building God's kingdom in Tamale and the surrounding villages. Mark and Johnson hit it off right away. Lydia and I became close friends almost overnight. We went to the market together, traveled to villages like sisters, cooked in each other's kitchens, and shared the gospel with the young girls in her sewing class. In short, we did life together.

One evening, when our husbands were out on evangelism, we saw a scorpion scurry across the living room tiles. We jumped up on the sofa and stayed there until Mark and Johnson got back. Johnson killed the scorpion with his shoe while Lydia and I clung to each other, giggling like helpless females—which we were at that moment.

Mark and Johnson made forays into nearby villages to lay the groundwork for ministering there. They and Eun Saeng (a fellow SIM missionary from Korea) asked the chief in one of the villages for permission to share a message from the Bible. When they returned the next week for his answer, they were amazed that the chief called everyone in the village to hear their message. Sharing from Luke 13:22–28, Mark explained he would discuss the basis on which the householder, God, receives some and tells others, "I never knew you, depart from me."

When Mark finished teaching, the village elders spent fifteen minutes deliberating. Then they brought their response: "We agree for you to come and teach us." No Christian group had ever come to this village. After that time, they met there weekly starting out with a crowd of about two hundred people listening intently. Each week the number of listeners decreased until there were about fifty people attending; many gave their lives to Christ. God opened up other villages to hear His message too and churches were being born.

God also provided avenues for me to teach women. "He said that?" my young friend Regina said when she heard Satan's account to Eve of the benefits of eating the forbidden fruit. I glanced up from my Bible and noticed Regina's astonishment. I realized this precious girl was hearing this story for the first time. I continued with renewed vigor, explaining the foundational truth of sin passing to all of us. At our next meeting, Regina gave her life to the Lord.

One of our many memorable new friends was a wiry fifty-year-old man. Alhassan came to know the Lord when he heard the gospel preached in his village. Hungry for the Word, he biked miles and miles over bush paths to reach the village where Mark and Johnson were teaching. Soon, he began faithfully sharing God's Word in his village.

By this time, multiple villages had fledgling churches meeting on Sundays. Johnson, Mark, Eun Saeng, and other evangelists started regularly teaching these spiritually-growing men at the Leadership Training Institute. The men would cycle from their villages every Tuesday morning and study God's Word together. Then, on Wednesday afternoon, they would return home to tend their farms and then teach what they learned in churches on Sunday.

Some of these pastors-in-training were unable to read and write, so they depended on their memories. The men in charge recruited me to join the staff to teach literacy. Alhassan was one of the first ones to be able to read the scriptures during class. God was growing His church one disciple at a time.

In February 1994, conflict between two of the largest ethnic groups erupted, resulting in many burned villages and deaths. Mark and two friends, Joseph and Sammy, received relief aid from non-governmental organizations to distribute to the refugees. Though Tamale had a refugee camp, 13,000 of the 14,000 displaced people they registered lived with relatives. African hospitality has no serious competitor.

Mark wrote in our newsletter on May 3, 1994: "The conflict seemed like a great setback for the work of evangelism. Interestingly, however, people who previously had refused to consider our message have not been able to ignore the wail of war and destruction that has humbled the land. Though God did not "sow" the war, He knew how to "reap" a harvest from it. The general Muslim population has been amazed that Christians have been so interested in their welfare. We are praying that many men and women will be added to the family of God."

We had lived in Tamale for eight years. In addition to the spiritual fruit from our move to Tamale, we also experienced God's blessing on our family: He entrusted us with two more children. I watched my three- and four-year-old adopted daughters play with their dolls. Both girls had been brought to the Tamale orphanage from their villages: Kinza from a village south of Tamale and Colette from a village north of us. Even though trials are inevitable, He gives blessings when we obey His direction.

"Madam Aisha!" my good friend Hellen called out to me as she walked up the path to our porch. She loosened the cloth securing her baby, Francis, to her back. I reached to take him and kissed his soft cheeks. Hellen squatted down to gather Kinza and Colette in her embrace. She fingered the girls' tight braids. "Who fixed their hair?"

"I did!" I said enthusiastically. Hellen had taught me how to make cornrow braids the African way. Like my interactions with Lydia, Hellen and I were also doing life together.

"Oh, Madam Aisha! Well done! You have graduated!" Our eyes danced in time with our hearty laughter as we sat down on the porch chairs and opened our Bibles.

I was having a fabulous time in this "armpit" of Ghana, the place of God's blessing for me.

James 1:25: But the one who looks into the perfect law, the law of liberty, and perseveres, being no hearer who forgets but a doer who acts, he will be blessed in his doing.

# Chapter Thirty-Two

# God Said No When I Needed a Yes

**March 2005 ~ New Orleans, Louisana**

I HURRIED DOWN THE crowded concourse to gate C14, clutching my standby ticket. I begged the Lord to get me on this flight. I had to get home tonight. Sighing with relief when I reached the gate, I collapsed into one of the pliable waiting chairs. I leaned on the handle of my purple carry-on, which I had pulled close to my legs, surveying the situation.

The waiting area was buzzing with about thirty impatient travelers, though the last group for boarding had been called—an ominous sign. My confidence was in the God of the universe, who could easily open a seat on flight 1354 for His child who wanted to get home.

Lord, I don't know what Your will is, but my will is to get on this flight to Columbus and then on to Milwaukee. Please, Lord. You can open the way.

"Final boarding call for flight 1354 to Columbus, Ohio," rang out over the loudspeaker.

No standby passengers were being called. Not a single one.

Flashing her dazzling smile to those of us waiting like puppies for a treat, the flight attendant closed the massive door with the finality of a coffin lid.

I couldn't believe God had said no to my prayer. I did what any disappointed child would have done in that situation: I cried.

Three days earlier, I had flown from Milwaukee to New Orleans to be with my dad and siblings. We were gathering for a family memorial service for my stepmom.

We found my dad and established contact with him when I was twenty-four years old, having just returned from Ethiopia. Five years later, Dad and Ginny married when we were on furlough from Ghana.

Ginny, twelve years younger than my dad, adored all four of us kids. Her favorite thing was to shop all year for Christmas gifts for us and our quivers of children (seventeen grandkids total). Kinza and Colette whooped joyfully when several big boxes arrived on our doorstep in Wisconsin during December—each package laden with many wrapped gifts.

My stepmom, who had been a heavy smoker, died of tongue cancer. I don't know if Ginny ever gave her life to Christ, but she always listened politely when we shared the gospel. My brother told me she said to him after he shared verses from Romans with her and our father: "That is what you believe, Rocky, but we believe differently than you." Two months after she said this, she entered eternity and learned the truth of what is on the other side of death.

The rain was pattering on the windows of the peach-colored Hotel Storyville in New Orleans. The five of us—Dad and us four kids—crammed into the closet-sized foyer for an intimate service.

Sitting on the hall steps, a small bench, and the floor, we shared memories of Ginny while my dad sobbed. I was grateful for this time—to pause our busy lives and reflect on a life that had touched us all while strengthening our bonds as a family. Grieving does that. Memorial services are for the living rather than for the one who died.

The next day, I watched my siblings pull their cars onto Esplanade Avenue to drive back to Georgia and South Carolina. Then I got into my dad's 1974 Cadillac for the wet drive to the airport. I insisted he drop me at the departure entrance—no need to pay for parking. We said our hurried goodbyes beside his open trunk, and I pulled my luggage into the terminal.

⟫⟫⟫ ⟪⟪⟪

I always savored my time at an airport once I was through security. I felt suspended in time—between my world of adventure and my responsibilities at home. The downside of air travel was the potential for delays affecting connecting flights. That was precisely what happened to me on this chilly March day.

Flights regularly took off from New Orleans, but my first connection in Atlanta was the problem. Atlanta had severe storms, and incoming flights were not allowed to land. My New Orleans departure was delayed until the weather in Atlanta permitted a safe landing.

I wasn't worried, though, as I had a few hours of margin between my Atlanta arrival and Milwaukee departure. I settled in with a book while waiting for the boarding call.

As the minutes became hours, I knew it was getting questionable that I would make my Milwaukee connection in Atlanta. I was hoping my flight to Milwaukee would also be delayed, giving me time to get there.

About five hours later, I landed in Atlanta. The inevitable had happened. My connecting flight was long gone. I joined the lengthy line of displaced passengers and waited my turn to be rebooked on another flight. The poor agent was frazzled and probably tired of dealing with irritable clients. But she cheerfully told me she could put me on standby on Delta flight 1354 to Columbus, Ohio, and then on to Milwaukee on the same plane.

Gratefully accepting the standby ticket, I was off in high spirits, weaving through other passengers hurrying to make their flights. I would get home that night after all.

My relief was short-lived when that flight took off without me.

And that is when I cried.

Gazing out the glass wall, I brushed away my tears as I watched Flight 1354 back away from the gate. I believed God would get me on that plane, but He had said no.

A dark cloud of sadness descended on me as I returned to the Delta service desk to get reassigned to another flight. My chances of getting to Milwaukee that night were getting washed away.

This time, I was assigned to a competitor's airline, Midwest flight 1566, which flew directly to Milwaukee. The agent handed me the standby ticket and told me to hurry—the flight would leave in twenty minutes. I didn't need to be told twice. I took off running. When I reached the assigned gate, I rushed to the desk and handed the agent my standby ticket, explaining my plight.

"Final call for Midwest flight 1566 to Milwaukee" rang out like a taunt to me over the loudspeaker. Out of breath and with my heart pounding, I waited for the magic words from the desk agent permitting me to board. But the young lady shook her head, making her ponytail bounce back and forth. "They can't do this. They know they can't do this. You will have to go . . ."

Her voice trailed off as she looked up at me, her blue-painted eyes meeting my mascara-smudged ones. Did she see my desperation . . . my message of "please help me get home"?

"Oh. Never mind. You can get on. There's a seat for you."

"Thank you!" I grabbed my boarding pass, which had spit out from her computer printer. "God bless you."

She chuckled at my reaction. "Enjoy the flight."

I watched Atlanta's night lights fading as we ascended to our flying altitude. It's good that Milwaukee is an hour earlier than Atlanta, so my husband wouldn't have to come so late to get me. Even so, it was after eleven p.m. when we landed.

It was exhilarating to arrive at my deserted hometown airport that night. Shops were closed, security podiums were vacant, and the clacking of my carry-on's wheels seemed to sing, "Finally home, finally home."

The one I loved was waiting at the end of the concourse with arms open wide. I was reminded of running into his embrace when I arrived in Addis Ababa thirty-one years earlier. The main difference between then and now was that our love had multiplied exponentially. I am blessed.

Hand in hand, we proceeded to baggage claim. We knew the drill: Stand strategically to grab the luggage as it is ejected. Watch as the moving belt journeys around the circle of travelers waiting for their bags. The duffel bags, trunks, and lots of brown and blue suitcases—some with ribbons on their handles—seemed to chase each other on the circular belt until their owners grabbed them off. We waited and watched, but my purple canvas suitcase never appeared. The belt groaned to a halt, indicating, "That's all, folks. There are no more bags from Atlanta."

Oh no! My luggage was missing.

We went to the baggage claim service desk agent and reported that my suitcase had not arrived. He nonchalantly entered my ticket information on his computer to locate my suitcase as if this weren't a big deal. I stood there, shifting my weight from one foot to the other while studying his face for signs of success in locating it.

"Your luggage was put on the flight to Columbus. The flight from Columbus to Milwaukee was canceled due to snow, so your luggage is overnighting in Columbus. It will be delivered tomorrow."

And then it hit me: if I had gotten on the flight to Columbus like I had wanted, I would have been overnighting in Columbus too!

Even though I didn't understand why God said no, He had my best interest in mind when He denied my request to get on that first flight. He planned to get me home that night and knew the Columbus flight would be stuck overnight.

God always knows best.

My will or God's will? I'll take God's will every time!

Proverbs 19:21 (NASB): Many plans are in a man's heart, But the counsel of the Lord will stand.

# Chapter Thirty-Three

# Hurting People Hurt People

**July 2008 ~ Hampton, GA**

I GLANCED AROUND THE semidark room with my family members gathered around the pastor, who had come to comfort us. He would preside over my father's funeral the next day.

My lone brother, Rocky, sat stoically on his favorite chair. He was the one who had discovered my father's fully clothed body in the tub. Rocky had made countless trips to New Orleans to assist my father in restoring his hotel after Hurricane Katrina. My brother chose to forget the devastating poverty my father had left my mother and us four young kids. He had generously brought him to live his final years under his own roof until my father decided otherwise.

My older sister, Anna, tired from her four-hour drive, leaned forward on her knees while perched beside her husband on the sofa. Her smeared mascara revealed her emotions even in the dim light. She was the closest to my dad and the most like him.

My younger sister and Mama sat with their hands clasped together as if secured by glue. When the three of us older kids were teenagers and trying our independent wings, Mama always had my little sister. Polly was her angel—sent by God to encourage Mama to keep going.

When my mother was asked why she drove 220 miles to her ex-husband's funeral, she responded, "Because all my children were going to be there. I wanted to be with them." She never held animosity against my dad, teaching us to love him and pray for him to come back. One time, Mama was interviewed by our state newspaper about life as a single mom. The reporter mentioned that we were a broken family, to which my twelve-year-old brother indignantly said, "We are not a broken family; we just don't have a daddy."

After clearing his throat, the pastor opened our small family gathering with prayer. He then began to speak about my father glowingly: He remembered the fishing trip the two of them had recently gone on and raved about my dad's golden voice belting out the hymns in church.

Quietly and carefully, I interrupted him. "It is appropriate for you to speak of our father as you experienced him; I am glad for your good times together. However, it is important to me that you not glorify my father in the remembrance service tomorrow. His choices during his life seriously hurt almost everyone in this room."

The pastor leaned forward as he considered this new information. He was well-groomed as an astute listener and was quickly able to redirect his words when the situation warranted it.

He asked each of my dad's four adult children if we had ever heard him say, "I love you." Each one of us responded no. I was surprised when my older sister also said no because she always wanted to be like our father. Even with that to her credit, it hadn't won her the longed-for words that every child wants to hear: "I love you!"

My dad had only one sibling, a brother who was twenty years younger than he was. For all practical purposes, my father was an only child. Soon after his brother, Boyd Stephen, was born, their mother died from cancer. My mom and dad had raised his little brother (my uncle) for five years, from when they were first married until my grandfather, Papa, remarried, taking his young son across the country. Sadly, we then lost contact with Boyd Stephen.

After many years, my mother located my dad's brother, Stefan, in California. (He had changed his name from Boyd Stephen.) Uncle Stefan and his girlfriend flew from California to attend his brother's memorial service in Georgia.

While Stefan drove us to the funeral, he asked me, "You know how you said last night that you never heard George tell you that he loved you?"

"Yes." That very thought was still burning in my soul.

"I got to thinking about that and realized that I never heard my dad say he loved me either," Stefan said.

And then it hit me like a wave knocking me down in the ocean: my father had never heard his dad say he loved him either. It was a parenting role that was not modeled for him.

During the funeral service, the dam covering my eyes gave way and the tears flowed. But I was not crying for my loss. I was crying for the loss that little boy in the 1930s felt—desperate for approval and love. He was never once told by his father, "I love you, son."

In that brief moment of understanding, my wounded heart became whole again.

And I was comforted.

Psalm 119:76: Let your steadfast love comfort me according to your promise to your servant.

# Chapter Thirty-Four

# When God Appointed a Deer

**September 2016 ~ Driving to Tennessee**

My older sister, Anna, was failing despite being on a respirator in a hospital in Tennessee. My other two siblings, Rocky and Polly, had been able to make the five-hour drive from Georgia several times during her decline.

Anna's husband, Kerry, held her hand for hours as the days turned into weeks. Her daughter-in-love, Mary, and her stepson, Jeremy, took turns by her side and read scripture to her. Her room was like Grand Central Station, with compassion, adoration, and care delivered with each incoming visitor.

One of her nurses leaned over all the breathing tubes, gently pulled back her dangling hair, and said, "You sure are loved!"

Anna seemed to be getting better until she decided to go to the bathroom alone one night. She fell and broke her hip. The next day, the orthopedic doctor examining her wanted to perform surgery. Her pulmonologist said, "Absolutely not—her lungs can't handle that trauma."

With this new crisis, it was imperative for me to travel to Tennessee if I was going to see my sister before she died. With my husband's blessing, I hurriedly packed the Yaris and began the trip south.

Once on the expressway, I took a deep breath to slow down my racing pulse. I settled into my lane and activated the cruise control. Even though autumn was soon to arrive, the trees were still lush with emerald green leaves. Occasionally, the concrete retaining walls were not continuous, giving access to the forest acreage along the highway's shoulder.

"I'm on my way," I said seemingly into the air, but I was chatting with my sister-in-love, Linda, on my speaker phone, clamped into its dashboard holder.

"That's great. Eleven hours is a long trip. Will you overnight on the way down?"

"Definitely. But I'm not sure where. I want to see how far I get today."

"Sounds good. Drive safely."

"I will. Love you. Bye." Click.

Wisconsin's I-94 boasted five lanes as I barreled south toward Illinois. I relished the quiet of being alone in the vehicle, with only the hum of the road accompanying my occasional singing.

On my right side, I caught a glimpse of a graceful deer bounding out of the woods toward the road, which was thick with traffic. She was about 500 yards ahead of me. All of us drivers slowed down, anticipating that she would probably run onto the highway.

I knew that someone was going to hit her, so I mentally prepared for slamming brakes in front of me or showers of a broken windshield glass to avoid. I lost sight of the majestic creature as I kept my focus on the road, slowing down more.

Then, BAM! The front end of my Yaris crumpled toward me as I was engulfed in the powder from the airbag deploying. I spotted the lifeless carcass spinning in circles in front of a semitruck on my right side.

My first thought was, "I hit a deer!"

My second thought was, "My airbag went off."

And my third thought was, "I'm not going to see my sister before she dies."

Trembling, I checked over my left shoulder to see if any cars were coming in the only lane between me and the center grassy median. Those drivers were probably in shock too, but they made it safe for me to move into their lane and off the road.

A considerate gentleman pulled over in front of me and rushed to see if I was all right. I grabbed my purse, phone, and laptop and quickly left the car, thinking it was on fire. But the "smoke" was just the chemicals from the airbag, so that was a relief—if a person can feel relief after hitting a deer.

I dialed 9-1-1, but when the dispatcher asked my location, I didn't know what to say other than southbound on I-94 past the Milwaukee airport. I handed the good Samaritan my phone, assuming he knew the closest exits and mile markers better than I did. A police car from a different jurisdiction stopped to help me until the sheriff from my jurisdiction could get there. The good Samaritan had provided my location, handed my phone back, and gone on his way since the police were now with me.

I called my husband to let him know of my accident and to come for me. I wasn't too far from his work—maybe fifteen miles. Except for being shaken up, I was unharmed, although I had been jerked about more than the human body appreciates. My headrest had protected my neck, and the airbag shielded my abdomen.

Best of all, this was not God's appointed day for my life on earth to end. He saved me from the deer coming through my windshield and killing me, which is known to happen when a compact vehicle collides with a deer.

I felt like the deer had been dropped in front of my car. I saw it coming from the forest and slowed down like the other vehicles. But then I didn't see it again until I hit it. It was almost like the deer had been "appointed" for me.

Why? To preserve me from a worse accident down the road? I don't know. But I know better than to question God's sovereignty in my life. I trust Him.

I was disappointed that I would not be able to see my sister before she died. Not being with my family to support Anna at this sorrowful time was distressing to me.

But years ago, on that mule trip, when I thought I had broken my back, I learned to recount all the good I could thank God for in that trial. So, I purposefully changed the direction of my musings from regret to thanksgiving.

I thanked God for sparing my life and for protecting me from serious injury.

I thanked God the accident didn't happen too far from Mark's workplace. He didn't have to travel hours to pick me up.

I thanked God that I could witness to the officer of God's goodness as he waited with me for my husband and the tow truck to arrive.

I thanked God that the tow truck driver was a young man who had defended my daughter in high school when she was being bullied. I was able to thank him again.

I thanked God for my extended family showing Anna such love and care. In this particular situation, I was not needed.

My body was weak. A precious doctor friend, Keren Rosner, advised a day or two in bed. She also brought me a meal.

I shifted my weight in bed as another sweet friend, Carol Batzko, entered my room. Mark had left the front door unlocked for her.

Carol sat on the edge of the bed and let me tell her the details of the accident. She also brought me a meal and prayed with me before she left.

I kept my phone by my side. Mary texted me photos of Anna to keep me up-to-date. Polly and Linda were my lifelines to know what was happening. Finally, on September 30, the incoming call, not a text, was from Polly, and I felt a wave of dread. I answered and heard her soft voice: "She's gone."

Anna's appointed day had arrived.

I thought back on the last ten days since my trip to show love to Anna was aborted. I remembered those who reached out to me in my trial to show their friendship and care for me.

And I heard the nurse's words to Anna echo in my heart: "You sure are loved!"

Whether one is in the process of dying or is prevented from being with the dying, the love of family and friends cushions the sting.

Hebrews 9:27: It is appointed for man to die once, and after that comes judgment.

# Chapter Thirty-Five

# Assignment: Steadfastness

**March 2014 (two years before Anna died) ~ Jonesboro, GA**

"Amy, would you please warm my shoes on the space heater?" my cancer-ridden mother pointed to the portable unit near her bed. She was living in my younger sister's home in Georgia. I had come from Wisconsin to spend a few days with her and take her to her oncologist appointment.

Her request jogged my memory of another time fifty years earlier of warming shoes.

Our natural gas was cut off after my father left us in January 1964 since we hadn't paid the bill. Mama heated the kitchen with the electric oven while warming our shoes on its open-door.

"It sure is cold in this house." I grabbed my blanket, wrapping it around my head and shoulders to ward off the chilly morning air.

Mama was singing in the kitchen, inviting her four chicks to enter with cheerful hearts. "Good morning, Glory," she said when she saw me joining my siblings at the shiny red kitchen table.

As she stirred the oatmeal, she continued her joyful attitude. "Isn't God wonderful to give us this oven so we can heat the kitchen and warm our shoes?" I glanced at the oven's open door, which had four pairs of shoes of varying sizes propped up on the racks so the heat was reaching the insides. I didn't think God was doing such a great job, though, because He was forgetting about our bedrooms.

Putting those toasty shoes on our feet was like an offering from Mama. It was as if she was saying, "I can't give you heated bedrooms today, but I can give you warm shoes." I smiled as she slipped my comfy brown shoes on my sock-encased feet, warming not only my feet but also my heart.

⇢⟫⟫⟩ ⟨⟪⟪⇠

I caressed that sentimental memory as I propped Mama's black orthopedic shoes against the heater. I positioned her shoes so the insides would be heated—like she did for me on those winter mornings when I was ten.

I thought of the verses in James 1:2–3: "Count it all joy, my brothers, when you meet trials of various kinds, for you know that the testing of your faith produces steadfastness." Mama was a living example of James's instruction to the believers. She had been through many trials where she consistently remained steadfast in her trust in God's goodness.

I glanced around her room at the reminders of God's work in our family. The pill bottles and syringes made me wince as I remembered the disease God allowed me to have as a child. Then I had to smile at how He had brought good from that with funds for my college education.

Wood-carved elephants decorated her dresser—a reminder of her visits to Ghana when we were missionaries. While in Kumasi, she had cooked from the matching pots that Donna had given me. Mama was the first to use our guest room, which we built by enclosing half of our verandah—the same room Sam slept in later when he stayed with us.

A stray toy van on the floor from her resident great-grandbaby made me chuckle. When Rob handed us the keys to their new Volkswagen van, Mama was there. And this transaction happened in the same driveway where some of her teenage students had thrown a firecracker at her.

The get-well cards on her dresser made me think of the congratulations card she sent us when we adopted Kinza. Her card welcomed our "treasure," the gift of another child to teach about Jesus. She had written inside, "Can't wait to meet this treasure." She didn't yet know the significance of the word "treasure" in Kinza's story, but there it was—right in her handwriting.

A muffled wince startled me from my reflections. "I'm ready for my warm shoes," she said with a radiant smile, even though I knew she was suffering from pain. It was time to leave for her appointment. I knelt before her to put her sock-encased feet into her toasty shoes—just like she had done to me fifty years earlier.

I knew that my eighty-three-year-old mother would soon be promoted from her earthly, decaying body to her heavenly one. I wasn't worried about losing her. She would be welcomed by her Boss, Jesus, to spend eternity with Him.

I have learned to trust God for His goodness to come through whatever testing He allows in my life. Trials are expected in our lives; God uses them to mature us. I want to allow steadfastness to have its full effect "so that the tested genuineness of your faith . . . though it is tested by fire—may be found to result in praise and glory and honor at the revelation of Jesus Christ" (1 Peter 1:7).

I pushed Mama's wheelchair to the reception desk in the oncology department. The nurse greeted her, "Hello, Mrs. Roth! I can see you are not feeling well today. I'll take you right back to the imaging room."

She took the handles of the wheelchair from me and began to push. Mama didn't miss a beat. Through her pain, she haltingly said to the sweet nurse, "Do you know my Jesus? He's been so good to me." Her voice trailed off as they turned down the hallway.

I raised my eyes heavenward as I recited Psalm 136:4 as a prayer: "God, You alone do great wonders; Your steadfast love endures forever."

Mama was put on hospice care. Soon afterward, my three siblings gathered at Polly's home so we could be together one last time before Mama died. Rocky came from Oklahoma, where he worked temporarily; Anna and Kerry came from South Carolina. I was there from Wisconsin. Some of Mama's grandchildren came too while I was there. Family love was palpable.

We told stories. We planned the funeral. We hugged. We cried. Unbeknownst to us at the time, our godly mother would enter eternity in only ten days, and Anna would follow her in two years. As a family, we were blessed to be able to celebrate Mama's life and cherish these moments spent together.

Gazing out the 747's window above the city of Milwaukee, I saw ribbons of streets winding through the high-rise buildings. Cars and trucks that resembled toys from my aerial view were darting about with no regard that my mother was dying. Not knowing when my mama's appointed time to go would be, I had returned home.

Only eight days earlier, I had said goodbye to Mark to spend time with Mama. God appointed those days to be Roth family days—showing love to Mama and embracing my siblings, their spouses, and their children. To be in the presence of the dying is a weighty feeling. But the more powerful uplifting feeling is joy that Mama, who had given her life to the Lord Jesus, would soon be completely healed in His presence.

It was time to turn my focus back to the assignments the Lord had for me in this next stage of life. I knew trials would still come my way, but I wanted to count each as an opportunity to glorify God.

I wanted to grow in steadfastness. That is my assignment. It is every Christian's assignment.

The pilot came on the intercom, but I wasn't listening.

I was landing in my current hometown where God has planted me for now.

I would see Mark very soon.

And I couldn't stop smiling!

James 1:12: Blessed is the man who remains steadfast under trial, for when he has stood the test he will receive the crown of life, which God has promised to those who love him.

# FINAL WORDS

Our daily lives are brimming with opportunities to worry. I once heard someone say, "I have a master's degree in worry!" Allowing worry to rule our emotions reveals a lack of confidence in God's sovereignty over what happens to us.

In Isaiah 64:8, God teaches us that He is the potter, and we are the clay; His hands fashioned us. Even though we are His handiwork, we still experience trials and hardships, which come from the reality of living in a fallen world. Damaged relationships, shattered expectations, ruined finances, and failing bodies can make us feel cracked and broken.

Have you heard of the ancient Japanese practice called Kintsugi? It consists of transforming broken pottery into a work of art by mending it with gold. The cracks of the fractured vessel become the focus of the restored one. After the repair, the "healed" scars, now seen in the gold seams, change the object into something unique and exquisite.

What a potent illustration of God's work in the lives of His children. Thinking about God healing our wounds with gold puts a fresh perspective on our trials. God brings beauty from them—splendor that glorifies Him. In Isaiah 61:3, we learn that the Spirit of the Lord anointed Jesus to give us the oil of gladness instead of mourning, the garment of praise instead of a faint spirit, that God may be glorified.

The choice is ours: We can be a child of God characterized by worry and doubt as we go through life, always asking, "What if?" and "Why me?"

Or we can embrace God's sovereign control of everything that happens to us. We can ask Him to help us learn from the trial, persevere through the hardship, and ultimately glorify Him for His goodness through life's storms.

God can empower us to change our worries into wonder. Because we have Jesus, we have everything we need to live a life devoid of worry and overflowing with the wonder of God's goodness.

Looking back in life's rearview mirror, we see God's goodness in the gold-filled scars. You have just read about some of mine. Thanks for joining me on this trip.

Remember the truths from Romans 8: God is for us, nothing can separate us from His love, and He works all things together for good for those who love Him.

May we see the gold in our mended vessels and glorify our Maker.

Rejoicing in the wonder of God's work in my life,
Amy Hagerup
Dousman, Wisconsin

# ENDNOTES

### *Chapter 1: Assignment: Loneliness*

1. SIM BEGAN AS the Sudan Interior Mission when sub-Saharan Africa was called Sudan. But when Sudan became a country in its own right, the name became a misnomer. It needed to encompass the scope of ministry across countries in the middle of Africa. Years later, SIM expanded to minister in Asia and South America. Although numerous names have been attached to the acronym SIM over the years, it is currently known simply as SIM International.

### *Chapter 2: Down to My Last Two Dollars*

1. Augusta Street Church changed its name to West Columbia Evangelical Church for a few years but later returned to its original name.

2. During one of our trips to Miango in Nigeria for our annual vacation, we visited Titus and Mary Ann Payne and their four children. God led me to Africa with the same mission as the Paynes.

### *Chapter 4: A Powerful Lesson from God's Provision*

1. My great aunt Anna T. was my maternal grandfather's sister. She would bring her delicious yeast rolls to every family gathering.

2. Aunt Anna T. also purchased annual passes to the Columbia Zoo so she could take her nieces, nephews, and their families whenever they visited.

## Chapter 5: I Can't Outgive God

1. Information on the drought in Ghana in 1983: https://www.ghanaweb.com/GhanaHomePage/features/Lest-We-Forget-1983-Thirty-Years-Ago-273736

## Chapter 6: Too Exhausted to Serve a Visitor

1. In 1997, we left Ghana and began a ministry with DiscipleMakers in PA, where we worked for four years. In December 2001, God moved us to Wisconsin, where Mark was missions pastor for five years.

## Chapter 7: Travel Didn't Go as Planned

1. We were given George and Marta's address but lost the small piece of paper when we had to evacuate Waka quickly. Sadly, we never had contact with them again.

## Chapter 8: Lesson Learned from a Mule

1. When we went on multiple-day treks, we used our limited number of disposable diapers for Benjy. We would burn the used diapers to avoid leaving any litter on the mountains.

## Chapter 9: Injured on a Mountainside

1. *Injerra bu wut* is the national food of Ethiopia. Injera is a flatbread made from the grain tef on a large griddle. It is served with wut, a

stew made from lentils, vegetables, or meat enhanced with spices. It is still our favorite ethnic food.

## Chapter 10: Dashed Expectations on Arrival

1. The Corwins arrived in Ghana three years later (July 1981), and we enjoyed working together in Kumasi for a few years.

2. We were on the last SIM charter flight because it was not financially viable for SIM to continue utilizing this method of air travel.

3. Cote d'Ivoire was the official name of Ivory Coast because the administration wanted the nation to be recognized by its French name.

4. Mark worked toward receiving his master's in missions from Columbia International University during our furloughs. Columbia Bible College (CBC) was the undergraduate division, while Columbia Graduate School of Bible and Missions (CGS) was the graduate division. Subsequently, Columbia International University replaced the original names.

## Chapter 11: How God Used a Vanity License Plate

1. Our son chose to attend Penn State rather than Mark's alma mater, the University of Illinois. Deeanne joined Ben at Penn State two years later. Heidi became a student and graduate of Columbia International University. Kinza graduated from Bradley University in Peoria, IL and received her masters in collaborative piano from Illinois State. Colette received her cosmetology certification from VICI Beauty School.

## Chapter 13: The Impact of the Family Boss

1. When Stefan was seventeen years old, my paternal grandfather, Amasa Boyd Roth, passed away due to a head injury sustained in a fall. At that point, we were not in communication with them.

## Chapter 14: Mama's Desperate Christmas Eve

1. Rhea F. Miller. "I'd Rather Have Jesus." Copyright 1922.

## Chapter 15: Doctor's Prediction I'd Go Insane

1. My piano teacher assumed Mama was discontinuing my lessons due to financial constraints. She told my mother she would teach me for free because she believed I was musically gifted. Mama never told me that part, but it probably wouldn't have mattered. I was too immature to let a future benefit outweigh the current discomfort.

## Chapter 16: When the FBI Came to Our House

1. John Newton. "Amazing Grace." Published 1779.

## Chapter 17: Letting Go of My Treasures

1. Julie Campbell wrote the first six Trixie Belden books. After that, the publishing house employed many authors to pen more stories under the pseudonym Kathryn Kenny. Out of the thirty-nine released volumes, fifteen are still available for purchase.

2. Campbell, Julie. *Trixie Belden and the Secret of the Mansion*. Toronto, Canada: Random House Books for Young Readers, 2012.

## Chapter 18: Reaction to a Hate Prank

1. "Good morning, Glory" was Mama's favorite greeting. She added "glory" to her "Good morning" as praise to God, not the flower. But I believe it was inspired by the flower "morning glory."

## *Chapter 20: Childhood Threads for God's Purposes*

1. According to my brother, Mama listened to these tapes recorded by Alexander Scourby. He was a well-known Shakespearean actor who rose to fame mainly as an audiobook producer. His rendition of the King James Bible is regarded as the best voice recording ever made of the text.

2. Elliott, Elisabeth. *A Chance to Die: The Life and Legacy of Amy Carmichael*. Old Tappan, New Jersey: Fleming H. Revell Company, 1987

## *Chapter 22: When Rose-Colored Glasses Were a Good Thing*

1. John W. Peterson. "I'm Not Alone." Copyright 1955 by Singspiration, Inc.

## *Chapter 24: A School Choice Dilemma*

1. Van Reken, Ruth E. *Letters I Never Wrote*. Oakbrook, IL: Darwill Press, 1987.

2. Our three oldest children completed their education at ICA. Even though it wasn't easy for them or us, we are grateful they matured in the Lord during their time there.

3. We humbly thank the Lord that all five of our children (including the two youngest who never attended boarding school) are continuing to walk with God and serve Him with their lives.

## *Chapter 25: When Our Kids' Valuables Were Stolen*

1. After our visit to Portugal, we stopped in Spain to see additional missionary friends. Marilyn, the wife, was the same young woman my mother had taught piano when I peeked through the door. Marilyn and I became life-long friends.

## Chapter 27: Jeered by the Spectators

1. When we were on furlough during our son's seventh-grade year, Benjy changed his name to Ben.

## Chapter 34: When God Appointed a Deer

1. Many years ago, I started referring to any in-laws as "in-love" because a legal connection results from a couple's love. So, I referred to Linda as my sister-in-love instead of my sister-in-law.

2. I thank the Lord that four months before Anna passed away, I spent five days in her Tennessee home where she lived with her husband, Kerry. We had precious time together, ordained by our Father, Who knew I wouldn't see her again on earth.

## Chapter 35: Assignment: Steadfastness

1. Ten days after I returned to Milwaukee, Mama was united with her Lord and Savior on April 14, 2014. We planned her funeral and burial in Columbia, South Carolina two weeks after her death. With our two youngest daughters, Mark and I drove south for the celebration of her life.

# ACKNOWLEDGEMENTS

I'M SO THANKFUL FOR the family God chose for me. Many thanks to my children, Ben, Deeanne, Heidi, Kinza, and Colette, who have blessed my life and supported me in sharing these stories that involve them also. I'm forever indebted to my brother, Rocky, for his invaluable help, support, and shared memories. I'm also in awe of Polly, my younger sister, who has been a dedicated cheerleader through all my writing. Thanks to my father's brother, Stefan, who has listened as I have shared with him long-distance. Thank you, Rocky, Polly, and Stefan, for allowing me to tell you my perspective of things that happened to you, too.

My heartfelt thanks to my Beta readers, Rocky Roth, Donna Andrist, Jamie Santana, Dan Smith, and Mary Kay Cleaver. Your encouragement, time, and invaluable feedback have been instrumental in shaping this memoir.

To my personal prayer team, Linda Nikitin, Kath Nikitin, Lori Barendsen, Gena Melang, Deeanne Maas, Mary Rebholz, and Donna Andrist, your prayers have been a source of strength and inspiration. I am deeply grateful for your support and thank God for you.

A special thanks to Liz Kenny, who repeatedly encouraged me to write another book. Many of my friends have also encouraged me with affirmations, telling me that they can't wait to read this book. Thank you all from the bottom of my heart.

I gratefully acknowledge every person in my stories whom God has used to help me grow in maturity and steadfastness—many thanks to those I could contact for permission to use their real names.

I am delighted to have been under the expertise of my editor, Pam Nordberg, and my cover designer, Angie Alaya. It was a pleasure working on my memoir with you two; you are the best.

I could not have finished this without the support of my husband and favorite person, Mark! I appreciate you being who you are, helping with memories, believing in me, and supporting and encouraging me. I love you, sweetheart. It is an honor to be doing life with you.

I bow in humble gratitude to my Heavenly Father, who is the mastermind behind every story in my life. All praise and honor belong to Him.

Finally, I'm grateful to you, dear reader, for your desire to grow in wonder at God's work in your life as well.

# ABOUT THE AUTHOR

Amy Hagerup is the wife of Mark, the mother of five blessings, the mother-in-love of five additional gifts from the Lord, and Nana of fourteen treasures. She is proactive about investing in her grandchildren's spiritual legacy, even though she lives far from eleven of them. Her life purpose is to help people take the next step in their spiritual lives.

In addition to her writing, she manages a Health and Wellness home business with her brand partner, Shaklee. She is known as the Vitamin Shepherd.

For those closest to her, Amy is known as a woman who loves Jesus, is passionately devoted to her family, and wants to please God in her daily choices.

You can connect with Amy, see photos of her family, read more of her stories, and learn about her health business at the following online places:

- Blog: https://amyhagerup.com

- Health website: https://VitaminShepherd.com

- Facebook author page: https://facebook.com/AmyHagerupAuthorPage

- Facebook group: https://facebook.com/groups/AuthorAmyHagerupPrivateGroup

- Instagram, Pinterest, Twitter, YouTube: @amyhagerup

# A LETTER TO THE READER

**Dear reader,**

Thank you so much for reading my book!

For a special video message from me and to join my email list, visit https://amyhagerup.com/welcome-video

Also to see the included book photos in color, go to https://amyhagerup.com/memoir-photos.

I appreciate your feedback; I love hearing what you say about turning worry into wonder and how God has worked well in your life.

I would appreciate your input as I continue to write and create more books for you.

Please take two minutes to leave an honest review on Amazon (or other book sites), letting everyone know what you thought of this book. This will help spread the message of God's goodness in all our trials, even when we can't see it yet.

Thanks so very much!

Amy Hagerup